IMMIGRANT BAGGAGE

Morticians, Purloined Diaries,
and Other Theatrics of Exile

Praise for *Immigrant Baggage*

"In Maxim D. Shrayer's extraordinary *Immigrant Baggage: Morticians, Purloined Diaries, and Other Theatrics of Exile*, he claims place through movement, expression through translingualism, all while inscribing history onto our collective present consciousness. Incorporating photographs into the stories of his travels and adventures, Shrayer offers eyewitness evidence of the past, even as his writing invites readers to marvel at improbable connections, surreal coincidences, and occasional forays into imagined endings that bring together past and present. An elegant and compelling narrator, Shrayer invites readers to visualize, understand, hear, and experience the richness of multiple languages, cities, and characters. He does this by inviting us not only to experience specific moments in time and place, but also to reflect on the spaces in between—indeed, it is in these moments that Shrayer seems most at home."
　　—Jessica Lang, Dean, Weissman School of Arts
　　　　and Sciences, Baruch College, CUNY and author
　　　　of *Textual Silence: Unreadability and the Holocaust*

"Maxim D. Shrayer writes like Nabokov's long lost cousin. Funny, poignant, elegant, and light on his feet, Shrayer serves up a banquet of émigré pleasures and sorrows, in the new world as well as the old. *Immigrant Baggage* is a compact, pang-filled, hilarious marvel."
　　—David Mikics, Moores Professor of Honors and English,
　　　　University of Houston, and author of *Stanley Kubrick:
　　　　American Filmmaker*

"The lively stories that comprise Maxim D. Shrayer's *Immigrant Baggage* burst with a passionate devotion to literature—the Russian literature of Shrayer's past, in particular, before he and his parents left Russia after eight persecuted years as Jewish refuseniks. Whether describing a literary discussion among friends from his Soviet youth, or among colleagues in America today, the conversations are of utmost importance; indeed, intellectual arguments can be loveable 'tirades' when the nature of literature is at stake. Poignantly, reading into this memoir familiarizes us with the texture of what it is to live exiled, as an immigrant, with one's mind perpetually in more than one world, and speaking more than one language. Shrayer's gift is to guide us, through his 'adventures,' to an understanding of the many meanings of the phrase *Immigrant Baggage*, including the inevitable weight of the past, the ever-present quality of being multicultural, and the literal need and desire to travel across the globe to stay connected to a world left behind. The son of a writer, Shrayer brings a certain wistfulness for the literary life of the past when he describes—to his daughters whom he lovingly shares his literary life with—his father taking him to editorial offices in Moscow and then for a treat of 'something delicious like a smoked tongue sandwich and pear soda.' The past is present, and made alive again, in this most engaging memoir."

—Elizabeth Poliner, author of *As Close to Us as Breathing* and *Mutual Life & Casualty*

"Maxim D. Shrayer is a faithful student of the great masters of Russian literature. And he is also top-of-the-class as a literary Russian émigré in his own right. This is a charming and breezy book, written by a wordsmith from two worlds—sparkling with the Soviet skepticism of a Jewish novelist who hasn't quite unpacked all his baggage in America, darting back and forth like a Nabokovian butterfly between locales, languages, and the Kafkaesque surprises and vexations of life."

—Thane Rosenbaum, author of *How Sweet It Is!* and *The Golems of Gotham*

"Maxim D. Shrayer has the sharp humor of a Russian literary outsider, the longings of a Jewish émigré, and the artistic discipline to examine his experiences without sentiment or shtick. Nabokov would have read this book with pleasure."

—David Samuels, literary editor of *Tablet Magazine* and author of *Only Love Can Break Your Heart*

"Maxim D. Shrayer is a precious object: a kind of living Rosetta Stone who embodies multiple literary cultures. In this compelling literary memoir, he moves between the stagnant decades of the late Soviet Union to present-day America, illuminating his tales with dazzling aperçus from the treasure-house of Russian-language literature. Shrayer's wry, witty, wise, and nuanced writing weaves together strands of Soviet, Russian, Jewish, and American culture in moments of translingual epiphany. Now more than ever, his work is a vital reminder of our common humanity."

—Marcel Theroux, author of *The Sorcerer of Pyongyang* and *Far North*

IMMIGRANT BAGGAGE

Morticians, Purloined Diaries, and Other Theatrics of Exile

Maxim D. Shrayer

Library of Congress Cataloging-in-Publication Data

Names: Shrayer, Maxim, 1967—author.
Title: Immigrant baggage : morticians, purloined diaries, and other
    theatrics of exile / Maxim D. Shrayer.
Description: Boston : Cherry Orchard Books, an imprint of Academic Studies
    Press, 2023. | Includes index.
Identifiers: LCCN 2022036367 (print) | LCCN 2022036368 (ebook) |
    ISBN 9781644699980 (paperback) | ISBN 9781644699997 (adobe pdf) |
    ISBN 9798887190501 (epub)
Subjects: LCSH: Shrayer, Maxim, 1967— | Immigrants—United
    State—Biography. | Authors, American—20th century—Biography. |
    LCGFT: Autobiographies.
Classification: LCC PG3487.R34 Z46 2023 (print) | LCC PG3487.R34 (ebook)
    | DDC 818/.603 [B]—dc23/eng/20220921
LC record available at https://lccn.loc.gov/2022036367
LC ebook record available at https://lccn.loc.gov/2022036368

ISBN 9781644699980 (paperback)
ISBN 9781644699997 (adobe pdf)
ISBN 9798887190501 (epub)

Earlier versions of sections of this book originally appeared in *Tablet Magazine*, *The Odessa Review*, and *Brown Alumni Monthly* in English and in *Degysta*, *Literratura*, and *Snob* in Russian.

All translations, unless noted otherwise, are the author's own literal renditions. All photographs were taken with the author's camera.

This literary memoir is a work of memory, recollection, reflection, and reconstruction. Some of the names of individuals and institutions as well as some of the dates have been changed or disguised.

Published by Cherry Orchard Books, an imprint of Academic Studies Press
1577 Beacon Street
Brookline, MA 02446
press@academicstudiespress.com
www.academicstudiespress.com

for Karen, Mira, Tatiana—
my guiding stars

Contents

Then Apolek completed the Last Supper and the stoning of Mary of Magdala. One Sunday, he unveiled the frescoed walls. Prominent citizens, whom the priest had invited, recognized Janek, the limping convert, in Paul the Apostle, and the young Jewish woman Elka, the daughter of unknown parents and the mother of many homeless children, in Mary Magdalene. The prominent citizens ordered that the blasphemous images be covered. The priest showered the desecrator of divinity with threats. But Apolek did not cover the frescoed walls.

—Isaac Babel

When I showed her pictures of paintings, she went directly to the figures as people, commenting on their physical characteristics and probable personalities. She saw rabbis in Greco, waiters in Grosz, greaseballs and gangsters and fairies in the groups of the Italian Renaissance.

—Edmund Wilson

Preface: Translingual Adventures

I had completed this book three weeks prior to the start of the war in Ukraine. Russia's invasion of Ukraine has placed—for the second time since my family's emigration/immigration—a demarcation line between my past and my present. In the spring of 2022, as I was putting the finishing touches to this book, I kept thinking of the bloodshed in Ukraine not only as an attempt by Putin's regime to murder the land where three of my grandparents had been born before the start of World War I, but also as a neocolonial war aimed at the restoration of the Soviet past.

In different ways, I'm rooted in three cultures—Russian, Jewish, and American. Yet a writer's life is about much more than one's sense of roots. It's about floating in spacetime, about the texture, scent, and taste of words. The war in Ukraine has brought into devastatingly sharp focus what I have known for quite some time and tried to practice in my work: writers are not only products of their origins but also creative remakers of their identities.

I first started thinking about the interrelationship of origins and literary language after coming to the West in the summer of 1987. The black sand of a seedy Tyrrhenian public beach in the Italian town of Ladispoli was my open-air reading and writing room. My parents and I had recently left Moscow for good after eight and a half years of a refusenik limbo. We were spending the summer in Italy while our US refugee visas were being processed. We had brought four suitcases, one of them containing three or four tattered family photo albums, and two manual typewriters, one my father's, the other mine. The typewriters have survived all the peripeties of transit and still function today, although not much besides those typewriters and some Russian books from our old Moscow library remains of the material baggage of our Soviet past. As to the memory of our lives before emigration, it's taken much longer to dispose of the immaterial baggage of exile.

It was a summer of transit, a time of many discoveries. In Italy, still waiting for America, I pored over books by Russian exiles who had faced the predicament of choosing another language of self-expression. First on my list was Vladimir Nabokov, the great Russian-American writer, author of *Lolita* and *Pnin*, who remade himself after coming to America as a refugee in 1940, having rescued his Jewish wife and son. I was also reading the novels and stories of Mark Aldanov, who wrote in Russian and actively published in English and who, in the 1940s and early 1950s, before the *Lolita* explosion, was the most commercially successful living Russian author in America. With me, copied into a small leather-bound notebook, was two-thirds of what would become my first poetry collection, to be published in New York in 1990. Would I ever be able to write in another language? I wondered that summer. What would be the price

13

of losing—of abnegating—what I thought at the time to be my own Russian voice?

Four months later, on a wet November afternoon of my first American autumn (which was balmy by Moscow standards), I walked across the campus of Brown University and knocked on the office door of John (Jack) Hawkes. Author of *The Passion Artist*, Hawkes was a legendary American postmodernist, the most famous writer on the Brown faculty. He was retiring the following year. A recent immigrant studying literature and literary translation, I desperately wanted to take Hawkes's last fiction-writing seminar. All the twelve slots were taken.

Silver-haired, witty, verbally perverse, Hawkes listened to my rambling account of leaving the USSR, of writing poetry and fiction in Russian, and of coming to the US. He waited, silently, lips twitching, then asked:

"Have you read Nabokov?"

Hawkes pronounced the first "o" in Nabokov's name with an extra roundness, as if caressing the stressed Russian vowel.

"Nabokov?" I asked, in disbelief. "Of course I have."

"He's remarkable," said Hawkes. "I first read him in 1945—in San Marino."

"My grandmother got lost in San Marino last summer," I commented. "She ended up on the local emergency radio broadcast."

Hawkes looked at me with bemusement. In 1965 his novel *Second Skin* competed with Nabokov's *The Defense* and Bashevis Singer's *Short Friday* for the National

Book Award for Fiction. Saul Bellow's *Herzog* took the prize.

Hawkes had no interest in Soviet politics, no ear for Jewish immigrant anxieties. Yet he let me into his fiction seminar as the thirteenth student and even had his own plans for my literary future. Hawkes wanted me to write surrealist, pathological tales set in the Russian countryside. In the spring of 1988, a translingual novice surrounded by other young writers—all of them American-born—I first tried my hand at composing fiction and nonfiction in English. I'm forever grateful to Jack Hawkes, whom I ended up disappointing with what was then my passion for politics-infused narratives.

Over thirty-five years have gone by. I've now lived in Boston much longer than in my native Moscow. Many times, over these years, I've asked myself, sometimes happily, sometimes wistfully, what it means to write translingually. I've learned that there's more to translingualism than working not just in one language but in two or more, simultaneously or consecutively. In the not so recent past, translingual writers used to be all alone, artistically homeless, culturally stateless. Think of the loneliness of Rahel, arguably the first modern Hebrew woman poet, who was born in 1890 in Saratov on the Volga and died in Tel Aviv in 1931, leaving for posterity two published collections of Hebrew verse and an unpublished manuscript of Russian poems. Think also of Paul Celan, a multilingual Jew from Northern Bukovina who lost his family during the Shoah, went on to write and publish peerless German-language poetry, and in 1970 killed himself in Paris. Think, finally, of the less unhappy yet still lonely story of Samuel Beckett, the Irish literary genius who spent much of his adult life in France and translated most of his French works into English. Is a translingual writer who has found a new home no longer writing in a trance, no longer living in transit?

Perhaps literary translingualism means, as the fervently monolingual American poet Robert Frost might put it, "betwixt and between," *both* here and elsewhere. If so, what happens when we discover a literary community of fellow translinguals? What changes when we perceive ourselves— and are perceived—as a trend, a literary movement, a school?

Let me turn, briefly, to the story I know best and sometimes call my own, that of ex-Russians—and ex-Soviets—writing in English. When the Russian diplomat Pavel Svinyin (Svenin) lived and published in Philadelphia in the 1810s, he was in a league of his own. When the Yiddish- and Russian-speaking Abraham Cahan, the legendary editor of the *Forward*, an immigrant from the Russian Empire, was learning to write fiction in English in the 1900s, he, too, did not have many interlocutors. The St. Petersburg–born Vladimir Nabokov had very few artistic colleagues in the truest sense of the word when he arrived in America.

In the 1970s and 1980s, many more writers came to the US and Canada from the USSR, riding the wave of the great Jewish emigration. These new Russian-American writers— Joseph Brodsky most famously—sought to write in English *Russianly,* and not so infrequently this ambition stood in the way of their styles and voices as they forded the Hudson and the St. Lawrence. It has taken at least a generation for Soviet immigrants to find their literary bearings in the New World, and perhaps even longer to form a translingual neighborhood—a community—both in their own eyes and in the eyes of the American and Canadian cultural mainstream. Some of today's translinguals left the former Soviet Union as children and young people. They—we—have their literary great-uncles and great-aunts on both sides of the Atlantic. Representatives of this new wave of American and Canadian translingualism write in English and do so by hearkening back to such major Jewish-Russian authors as the incomparable short-story writer Isaac Babel and also to Ilya Ilf and Evgeny Petrov, who coauthored their popular satirical novels. At the same time, not surprisingly, some of the Russian-American authors also nominate Bernard Malamud, Philip Roth, and Mordecai Richler as their literary ancestors. Today we have translingual literary lovers and partners, editors and publishers, friends and next-door neighbors. A greater sense of shared cultural ancestry and thematic unity makes the circle of today's Anglophone writers from the former USSR something of a Russian family business and also something of a Jewish community affair. Only time will show whether we're bound to lose our Russian-American and Russian-Canadian voices tinged with a Jewish accent.

Over the years of living—and writing—away from Russia, I have gone through periods of writing literary texts only in Russian, of writing no literary texts in Russian, of writing poetry in Russian and literary prose in English, and of writing only literary prose in English. The final year of the Trump rule and the onset of the COVID pandemic led me to the composition of English-language poetry, some of it in the satirical mode. And throughout these years of living as an émigré and a translingual subject, I have always been involved in one or another form of self-translation. Self-translation has evolved from attempts to give previous Russian texts another life in English (a life they may or may not have deserved)—through creatively revising my English-language fiction and nonfiction—to parallel compositions of texts in both English and Russian, a mode that I presently find most stimulating.

In what language do you think? I'm often asked during readings and literary events. Is it Russian? English? Both? I reply, honestly, that in a sense it does not matter for the creative outcome. Over the years, I have had vivid dreams in which I lectured in French about sophisticated matters of culture and history. When I'm awake, my command of French is limited. In the spring of 1993, when I was living and doing research in Prague, I experienced dreams in which I had extensive debates about politics with the former vintage 1968 Czech dissidents. In reality, my Czech is quite rudimentary. I'm pointing this out because dreams give us deeper access to mechanisms of culture production—mechanisms that probably impact translingual writers most profoundly by revealing the hidden texture of exile.

To return to one's translingual beginnings, my 1987 experience as a Soviet refugee in Italy eventually informed the writing of the literary memoir *Waiting for America: A Story of Emigration*, in which discoveries of new worlds—

and words—are measured on the rusty scale of nostalgia. Other books of literary nonfiction and fiction have followed, including *Yom Kippur in Amsterdam*, *A Russian Immigrant: Three Novellas*, and the memoir *Leaving Russia: A Jewish Story*, first composed in English and subsequently recreated in Russian. Three and a half decades after emigrating from Russia, and now feeling less of a stranger among American writers, I'm still discovering the pleasures of writing in tongues.

An immigrant's life is always and inevitably a story of unburdening oneself of the past and a history of border crossing. The borders—or boundaries—include those of languages, cultures, and countries, some of them invisible while others still guarded with silences or even barbed wire. And the attempts at border crossing sometimes delight or enchant the transgressor while also auguring disappointment, heartbreak, or even real danger.

Composed in the time of the COVID-19 pandemic, this book of translingual adventures is but a partial record of my immigrant discoveries, transgressions, and valedictions.

—M. D. S.
February 2021–March 2022; June 2022
Chestnut Hill–South Chatham, Massachusetts

Immigrant Baggage

It all started in the winter of 2017. Visualize the sun of Veneto, end of February in Verona, and a happy Russian immigrant who had just arrived in Italy with his family from a wintry Boston. Ahead lay a sabbatical, a few lectures at Italian universities for me and a medical conference for my wife, but mainly a respite from taking call (for my wife) and from students ever ready to chew off their professor's liver (for me). Little compares in its fullness to the pleasure of recognizing the Italian beauty that we had first tasted as twenty-year-olds, Karen as a Henry-Jamesian American girl abroad, I as a Soviet refugee waiting for America. And now we planned to reconnect with all this visual and sensual plenitude, not alone but in the company of our daughters Mira (aged eleven at the time) and Tatiana (who was ten). It took us a day and a half to pose on Juliet's balcony, see a performance of *I Capuleti e i Montecchi* at the local opera house, stand on the arched bridge over the Adige (from which one observes the ruins of a Roman theater and the winged kayaks venturing to rise against the vernal waters), and perform a slow reading of the menu cards at Verona's trattorias. On the evening of our second day, amid the *dolce far niente* we never practice back in Boston, I gave a talk at the local university. I spoke about the (mixed) marriage of V & V—Véra Slonim and Vladimir Nabokov, and my host was Count Stefano Aloe in a great black beret, friend of poets, philosophers, and itinerant musicians. On the morning of 21 February 2017, my wife, daughters, and I squeezed into a red Fiat and drove up to the Dolomites, where ahead of us lay eight days of skiing.

I won't get into the journey from Verona to the former South Tyrol (for which Himmler had special plans) and the brief stop in Bolzano, where my daughters saw famous Ötzi the Iceman, who is almost five thousand years old. If you've been there, my description won't surprise you, and if you haven't—take my word. Just the archeological museum alone justifies a visit to Bolzano. The museum and also a glass of the local Lagrein, in which one hears the guttural notes of the Ladin language laced with an echo of millennia. Why the Ladin language? Because our route took us to the heart of Ladin history and culture. In German this autonomous region of Italy—something of a bridge between central and southern Europe—is called Südtirol, and in Italian it bears a longer name, Trentino-Alto Adige. Lover of minorities and autonomous districts that I am, I was especially drawn to the ancient tribe of Ladins, proud descendants of the Raeti, whom the Romans colonized at the start of the common era. As I planned the trip to the Dolomites, I purposefully chose the village of Badia, the northernmost and farthest in the Alta Badia chain of ski resorts. I so wanted to immerse myself in the life of this Ladin village, to hear the ancient language and observe the ways of this small European people, which numbers about 30,000 altogether.

At the sunset hour, we had left behind the villages of Colfosco, Corvara, and La Val and entered the village of Badia, located in the foothills of Santa Croce. When translated from the Italian, our hotel bears the name Mountain Melody or Melody of the Mountains, and in the original this name didn't scald our ears with banality but instead offered a promise of harmony. The front of the hotel faced the ski slopes; its back, the snow-covered hills, overgrown with pines and studded with dairy farms. From afar, our hotel resembled an early flying machine. Each room had a balcony, each offered a special view or vista.

"The Magic Mountain," I said to my wife as we stepped onto our balcony for the first time.

Karen had read Thomas Mann a long time ago and forgotten who in the novel recovers and who becomes ill. Whereas I could never forget …

For many years the hotel had been in the same Ladin family, and its matriarch, a nonagenarian *signora*, served the afternoon *glühwein* and home-baked cakes. Most of the hotel employees were local villagers, the majority of them Ladin. And only the tall bartender hailed from a town near Trieste. Dinner at the hotel was elevated to a four-act culinary

spectacle. Everything in the hotel immediately struck us as elegantly and thoughtfully arranged. This was a place one fell in love with and wanted to stay at for the rest of one's life—both the hotel and the mountain village. There was just one circumstance ... On the afternoon of our first day, we encountered several Germans and Austrians in the hotel sauna.

"Don't you like Garmisch or St. Anton?" my wife asked the fellow steamers.

"Here snow is better, and German is also spoken," a smiley gentleman from Munich replied in English. "But most of all, the food. This Edenic food!"

The next morning, after having rented skis and helmets, Karen and I had left the girls for half a day at Scuola Sci Badia. We had finally taken the chairlifts to the top of Santa Croce. It was an ideal day for skiing. Windless, sunny, perfectly groomed snow without icy bald spots of the sort one can rarely escape in New Hampshire or Vermont. We went down twice, ascended the mountain for the third time, and decided we would each take a different run and meet at the bottom.

In a state close to levitation, I was gliding down a wide, uncrowded slope. The next several minutes stand before my eyes in slo-mo. I registered, with some sort of an extreme side vision, how a silver arrow flew straight at me. I remember a red ink blot in the upper left corner of the frame. Then I remember falling down and the slope rotating as my skis shot off. And after that I remember feeling a beastly pain in my left flank. And the face—contorted with malice—of a snowboarder who had lost control as he turned. He looked about forty-five, and as is often the case when all one's senses are at their sharpest, I have forever remembered his frogskin face, shaved so clean that it looked as if it had been splashed with sulfuric acid. The snowboarder had unfastened his boot strap, moved closer to me (back then we didn't think about distancing), straightened the silver-framed glasses sitting askance on his small nose bridge, and said in English:

"You made the wrong turn."

This is verbatim what he said.

With difficulty I got up from the ground and looked first at the bottom of the lift, where antlike life was swarming, and then at the horizon lined with fleecy clouds.

"How can one 'make the wrong turn'? What kind of nonsense is that?" I pressed out.

"You made the wrong turn, and we collided. You could have killed me," the snowboarder attacked.

"How long have you been snowboarding?" I asked.

"This has nothing to do with the matter," the snowboarder wouldn't budge.

I felt an urge to smash his nose.

"You rammed into me at full speed," I said, trying not to scream in pain. "I probably broke my ribs, and you haven't even tried to apologize or ask if I needed help."

"I have nothing to apologize," the snowboarder said triumphantly. "And I see that you're okay if you can get up by yourself."

"Are you a doctor?" I asked for some reason.

"Neurosurgeon," the snowboarder answered.

I've seen him somewhere ... *doctor-death*, flashed through my head. At that moment I noticed an elderly spry skier in a sky-blue jacket who was step-laddering up the slope toward me. The last thing I need now is an SS man in retirement, I thought as a feeling of revulsion for all of humankind possessed me. In reality, the elderly "SS man" revealed himself to be a lovely old man from Stuttgart, who immediately took my side.

"I saw everything. Entirely your fault," he said in German into the tightened face of the snowboarder who had injured me.

"He drove straight into you. Very, very dangerous," the old gentleman added in English and extended his right hand to me.

The snowboarder quickly collected a semblance of a smile on his face and offered to help me with finding my skis and getting down the slope.

"I don't need your help," I replied.

The Dolomites are different from the East Coast ski resorts where first-aid patrols are common on the slopes. And so I had to overcome the pain and ski down, which took about twenty minutes. Karen was waiting at the lift entrance. Next to her stood the German snowboarder, rubbing his shoulder with affectation.

"He told me," said my wife, kissing me. "Where does it hurt?"

"It hurts like hell in my left flank," I answered. "I think it's the ribs."

"The ribs will eventually heal. We need to rule out a ruptured spleen," Karen said confidently.

"And by the way, how did he figure you out?" I asked.

"No idea. He came up and told me you fell and hurt yourself. He's a doctor from Berlin."

"And that you had rammed into me at full speed? Did you tell my wife?" I asked the snowboarder.

"Colleagues, let's not argue. You must quickly see a doctor," the neurosurgeon said, his voice unctuous.

There I was, standing in a half-stupor at the bottom of Santa Croce. My wife had run to the ticket office and quickly came back.

"I called for a car to take us to Bolzano," Karen reported. "There's a hospital there."

The snowboarder waved to us with the fingertips of his right hand.

"I hope is nothing serious," he said. "Feel better."

"By the way, what's your name?" my wife asked.

"Dr. Becker," the neurosurgeon replied.

"And your first name?" my wife added to her question.

"Ludo," he hesitantly added.

Atta girl, I said to myself. The most important thing in life is to marry well.

The taxi driver, a huge fellow with a bristly glistening face and blackened fingers, turned out to be neither Italian nor Ladin but a German-speaking Tyrolean.

"Why do you want to go to Bolzano?" he asked.

"Where else can we go?" I asked.

"I'll take you to La Villa to see Dr. Martin," the driver suggested, speaking in German. "Just five kilometers from here."

"Is he any good, your "dochtorr Mahrrtin"? I queried, impatiently.

"Delivered my three children. My wife thinks he's the best in the region."

Ten minutes later, we were standing in the reception area of the office of "Spechtenhauser Dr. Martin. Praxis für Allgemeinmedizin."

"To fill out paperwork. To wait near two o'clocks," said the lady from the reception window.

"Do you have all the equipment?" I asked.

"You will go to *Röntgen*, and if necessary, to get other tests. Now to sit and wait."

While Karen had gone out to fetch us sandwiches and coffee, I studied the waiting area. Sitting in it: a pregnant woman, a boy with crutches, a very petite old lady all in black, next to her a very old gentleman in a Tyrolean hat with a green feather, and, finally, a burly man, his right arm in a sling. (He told me he was from Erfurt, originally from Kherson.)

Dr. Martin Spechtenhauser was a tall, athletically built man with a barrel mustache. Not so much through the likeness of stature but rather with the fleeting expression of aged sadness one sees on the faces of circus performers, Dr. Spechtenhauser resembled W. G. Sebald, that most tender of German memoirists who had spent much of his life in England and died in his car on a rural road.

"Well, let us look," said Dr. Spechtenhauser.

"First we X-ray," he said to my wife. "Then we ultrasound. Please wait in reception area."

"I'm actually a doctor," my wife objected.

"Would you like to take my place?" asked Dr. Spechtenhauser, not in a rude but in a tired voice.

Karen didn't argue and left the exam room.

A technician did the X-ray, but when it came to the ultrasound, Dr. Spechtenhauser stepped in.

"Broken, broken," he announced, inviting my wife to come in. "But the spleen is intact."

At the reception window, they gave me a plastic sleeve with a note stating the diagnosis: "Fraktur der X Rippe und knöcherne Infraktion der XI Rippe Hemithorax links." Inside the sleeve were also copies of the imaging, a prescription for painkillers, and the paid bill for 330 euro.

I returned the ski equipment. At the lift ticket office they refunded me—in cash—for most of the weekly pass. Cursing fate, I returned to the hotel, undressed, and studied the livid-purple bruises descending, like tongues of molten lava, from my left flank across the hip down my left thigh. I ran a bath, took a swig of bourbon from a flask, and tried to relax. Except I couldn't shake the thoughts about universal justice.

Before stretching out on the red sofa, from which I had a partial view of the snow-powdered firs, I flung open the laptop and fed to Google the words "Dr. Ludo Becker" and "Germany." I immediately got my answer. A Dr. Ludo Becker worked at a private surgical clinic in Wannsee. I clicked on the link, and the swampy eyes of the snowboarder who had crashed into me looked out through a film of mire. I only had the strength to type a very short email: "Dr. Becker, I attach a copy of the diagnosis and bill. I hope you won't mind compensating me for the medical expenses. Yours, MDS." Already before going to bed, after supper with my wife and daughters (who would ski without me for a whole week), I checked my email to discover the following reply: "Mr. S., for me the ski season is also over, my rotator cuff is torn. You broke your ribs through no guilt [sic] of mine. But still I forward your information to my insurance company. They shall contact you. L. Becker."

In 1991, when I first started reading Nabokov in a serious way as a first-year doctoral student at Yale, I found his Russian quatrain, composed in March–April 1950 during a bout of intercostal neuralgia, to be too mannerish: "O no, those aren't ribs,/ — this pain, this hell fire —/ those Russian strings/ still ache in the old lyre." At the end of February 2017, I saw these translingual verses in an entirely new light, now appreciating their precision. For the first two nights after the accident on the ski slopes, I couldn't sleep prostrate. I would sit in an armchair by the balcony door, staring out at the hills, silver-sprinkled with fresh snow. Then I got used to it and let the new fractured rhythm of life take hold. I had breakfast in the morning with Karen, Mira, and Tatiana. (Instead of ham, Raffaella, our compassionate server, would bring bresaola or smoked turkey.) I would then walk my family to the shuttle stop and set out on a long stroll around the village of Badia, making frequent stops to marvel at the details of carved windows and doors, at the deer grazing on frozen grass right below one of the chairlifts, at happy horses and cows at a farm adjacent to our hotel. I even tried to compose something or to edit drafts of what I'd written just before leaving Boston for Italy. Every day I took lunch at Ustaria Posta, a Ladin restaurant where at noon the local men would gather at the bar for a dram of grappa. I, too, would have grappa.

Strong painkillers prevented me from thinking clearly. I submitted a short piece about Moscow circus clowns with Jewish names to a popular New York–based magazine with a Jewish slant. After it came out, it was discovered that, by mistake, I had included a chunk of text from an essay that had been published in another New York–based magazine serving Jewish-American readers. I had to do a whole lot of apologizing, and to this day the editors of the second magazine haven't forgiven me …

The pain subsided after a couple of weeks, and I even drove a car and carried suitcases down narrow Florentine alleys. And I didn't much regret not having been able to ski.

We returned to Boston at the end of March, and I was prepared to leave the whole incident with the Berlin neurosurgeon at the trash heap of memory, but easier said than done ... An envelope from Germany was waiting in our mailbox. It was a long letter from attorney Dr. Christian H., who represented Dr. Becker's insurance company: "I was assigned to handle the case in connection with the incident at the Santa Croce mountain in the region of Alta Badia." The letter contained detailed instructions. I was to provide "a description of what transpired on 22 February 2017 along with a plan to the area" [sic] and a step-by-step explanation. Only after that, attorney H. stated, "we would be able to investigate the issue of compensation of 330 euro."

I have trouble with questionnaires and long insurance forms. Back in the summer of 1993, during my first trip back to Russia after emigration, I interviewed Leonid Leonov, a wonderfully gifted fiction writer and playwright but hardly a friend of the Jews. Among the pearls of wisdom the ninety-three-year-old writer shared, two have stayed with me: "I've always had good relations with *them*" (about Jews) and "I belong to the unfortunate cast of so-called stylists who take two weeks to compose a simple acknowledgment, 'I received three rubles from. ...'" And so I struggled with the stupid German insurance explanations. I wasted half a day on the composition of the required answers, appended copies of all the necessary forms to my letter, and mailed it all to Germany. I telephoned my own insurance company on the same day, only to find out that they would compensate me for the overseas medical expenses, but I would have to get another X-ray (which they would cover). More dogged gibberish, I thought to myself, translating a Russian idiom, yet made an appointment for additional imaging. As luck should have it, the radiologist who read my film was our family friend Dr. Sabina B. She was born in the town of Orhei, also the homeland of the Jewish poet Dovid Knut and of Meir Dizengoff, the first mayor of Tel Aviv. Hence their shared sense of Bessarabian Jewish humor. Sabina called me to say that I was "beautiful inside," but I had not two but actually four broken or fractured ribs. "They are healing now and will be stronger in the end," Sabina added.

Two or three months later came the second letter from attorney Dr. Christian H. It stated that I had not provided exact details—where I was skiing from and to, at what speed, what the meteorological conditions were, and, most importantly, if there were witnesses to what transpired. I was really furious but forced myself to reply. Naturally, I didn't have the name of the charming old "SS man" who "saw everything" and would be able to corroborate that the incident was "entirely" Dr. Becker's "fault." And so I had to state that an elderly gentleman from Stuttgart (such and such details of appearance and clothing) was there, but I hadn't written down his name or contact information because I was in a lot of pain. In a follow-up letter, which arrived in another month or so, attorney H. notified me that "an unnamed old gentleman from Stuttgart was not acceptable to serve as a witness to establish what transpired" and that in order for the insurance company to continue the investigation I would need to supply additional information.

"Why do you need this?" asked my wife. "They've already reimbursed us."

"What about justice? What about fairness?" I replied with a question.

"The world is not a fair place," Karen said. "I'm sorry."

"I can't just give up," I said to my wife. "I just can't. The rat ruined our whole trip."

My wife knew me to be inconsolable about certain things.

In my reply to attorney H., I expressed a particular view of bureaucracy, as well as pointed out how absurd it was that for his services the attorney would probably charge five times the amount of the compensation I asked for. It was one of the worst letters I've ever written and sent. I mailed a copy to Dr. Becker's office in Wannsee. Let him gorge on it, I thought, waiting in line at the post office in Chestnut Hill—on the way to my university.

Three years went by. For my fiftieth birthday, my family took me back to the Dolomites. We stayed in the same hotel in Badia, and every day I looked for Dr. Ludo Becker on the slopes. The following year we returned to the Dolomites, and I was still hoping to confront the snowboarder with swampy green eyes. I've learned from this experience that we're not only drawn to scenes of crime or places of first love. We're also drawn to sites where we might run into our past offenders.

I'm typing these lines on 16 December 2020 at our family dacha in the village of South Chatham on Cape Cod. This is where we had sheltered in place during the worst months of the COVID-19 invasion, and we escape to the dacha from Boston at every opportunity. Ours used to be a very quiet pocket of the Cape, especially off-season, but the place has changed over the year of the pandemic. In two houses just around the corner from us, refugees from the pandemic have taken shelter: a couple of musicians who can no longer tour and also a Jewish poet and his wife, an archeology professor from the Bay Area. The village feels livelier but also more crowded with people. It's the seventh night of Hanukkah, and a nor'easter is fast approaching. The girls and I are talking about going skiing to New Hampshire for a couple of days. My wife cannot go because of her medical work and travel restrictions but also because after the Dolomites it's hard to get excited about New England skiing. But I feel that we can't be too choosy during a pandemic.

Now imagine my bemusement when I received another letter from Dr. Christian H., the attorney for the German insurance company. The letter "formally notified me" that because I had not "supplied the requested information concerning the ski incident of 22 February 2017," the compensation procedure was now permanently closed due to "lack of evidence."

Romance with a Mortician

Hung above the gates there was a sign depicting
a corpulent cupid holding an upturned torch in his hand
and the words "Sold and made to order here are coffins
simple and painted, and old ones are let and repaired."

—Alexander Pushkin

I have observed two varieties of morticians: the jovial and the tenebrific. The first type are the amateur humorists who have the talent to live with ease and to lay others to rest with such panache that it looks like they are sending them off to a holiday celebration. The second type are the professional mourners who walk through life with the stamp of martyrdom and bury people with such scorn that the survivors feel guilty for not having chosen a more expensive funeral.

This story has a double preamble. Double—because strands of my Moscow Soviet past have woven themselves into a thick braid of immigrant American living …

In 1987–1989, my first two years in America, I had the exquisite habit of visiting the periodicals room at the Rockefeller Library of Brown University. Once a week I would go there, sit in a deep swivel chair by the window, and peruse

Russian-language newspapers and magazines, both émigré and Soviet. At the time, the largest émigré daily was the New York–based *Novoye russkoe slovo* (New Russian Word), to which I began to contribute essays and stories. For some reason the editors liked to place the ads for celebratory events and funeral parlors on the newspaper's "literary page." I remember seeing awkwardly rhymed ads for the services of an actor, formerly of Moscow, whom I had met in Italy while our families waited for US refugee visas. In New York the actor specialized in hosting parties:

> Bar Mitzvah? Jubilee? A wedding?
> Call now and book, no need for waiting.
> I guarantee you joy and love.
> Your party host,
> *Pyotr Perchikov.*

And I also recall the stylish ads placed by two undertakers competing for the bodies—if not the souls—of Russian Jews in America. The first, Jack Yablokoff Funeral Home, had been founded in the 1960s by the son of the Yiddish actor Herman Yablokoff, writer of the famed song "Pipirosn" about an orphaned Jewish boy who sells cigarettes on city streets. The second funeral business, Wolk Memorial Chapels, had been established in the 1980s by a Soviet émigré of the same wave as the one writing these lines. The ads by the latter funeral service made mention of a (Dostoevskian, to my ear) "catalog of coffins." By the early 1990s, I had stopped reading *New Russian Word* or contributing to it, and after moving to Boston in 1996 I interacted less frequently with émigré literary circles.

The second circumstance had to do with my old Moscow friend Sasha Beyn. Sasha was five years my senior, and back in 1979, when our distantly related families became refuseniks and befriended each other, Sasha was a college freshman. In my eyes of a Soviet six-grader, he embodied Jewish strength and zealotry. Sasha grew up in a rough area of Moscow, worked out in the boiler room with a group of bodybuilders, and wasn't afraid of walking around with a Star of David on his neck. The Beyns left in 1981, just as the curtain of the great Jewish emigration was about to fall, and my parents and I remained refuseniks for six more, long years. Sasha didn't have the softest of landings in America. He first worked at a greenhouse, then at a gym, then delivered pizzas, and only eventually was he able to transfer his Soviet credits and return to college. Several years later he got into law school and gradually built a thriving real estate practice. Sasha married late, in his fifties, and by a small coincidence I'd met his wife Deena—now the owner of a swanky boutique on Lexington Avenue—in the days of our Moscow youth, at the apartment of my close friend Max Krolik. Even though Sasha Beyn and I live in different cities and don't see each other often—and despite the Trump-era politics that put many a wedge between Russian immigrant friends—Sasha and I have retained each other's affection and trust. Which finally brings me to the events at the tender heart of this story.

In the spring of 2018, I was invited to speak at the launch of an anthology of Russian-language prose and poetry in honor of Israel's seventieth anniversary. It was published in New York under the curatorship of Gennady Gatsov, now a TV personality, but always a poet and essayist and one of the pulsating coordinates of the Russian-American cultural landscape. It was an ambitious volume featuring three generations of writers. I have known some of the contributors for decades: an attorney from Chicago who has become an ardent Ukrainian nationalist; a poetry translator who has given the English language almost the entire oeuvre of Osip Mandelstam; a feminist thinker best known for her long ode to the brassiere; a pathologist who cultivated the

translations into English. In our family, Tatiana is a fourth-generation writer, and I have always tried to take her to various literary events and gatherings. When I was a kid in Moscow—this was before we became refuseniks—I used to hang out with my father and his fellow writers, and it made me understand much about the thing they used to call a "literary life."

The hotel where we stayed had a soothing name, The Lucerne. During the first peak of the COVID-19 outbreak, in July 2020, the city would temporarily expropriate this old Upper West Side *petite dame* and turn it into a homeless shelter, much to the chagrin of some of the local residents. However, the events I'm describing took place more than a year before the pandemic, when life seemed more immune to epidemiological catastrophes and when Trump appeared to represent a greater threat to the liberal imagination than the ever-mutating strains of the deadly virus. At the time, at least to my internal Russian exile, the name of our hotel brought to mind Tolstoy's story, in which the main characters stay in Lucerne's "finest" hotel: "When I went up to my room and opened the window onto the lake, the beauty of this water, these mountains, and this sky literally blinded me in the first instant. I felt inner anxiety and the need to express somehow the surplus of that something suddenly having overflown my soul. At that moment I felt a need to embrace someone, tightly, to embrace, tickle, pinch, and in general do something extraordinary with that person and with myself." When Tatiana and I pulled apart the shades in our room at The Lucerne, we saw the gaping purple well of the inner courtyard, ribs of construction staging dotted with plastic buckets. At the same time, there was a nice bistro, Nice Matin, down below at the corner of Amsterdam and 79th, and just a couple of blocks away—the Museum of Natural History, where Tatiana and I headed after a late breakfast with crispy croissants and "runny eggs," as she would later write in a poem.

Once at the museum, I followed Tatiana to the Hall of Human Origins, where skulls and skeletons of our ancestors and near-ancestors bear witness to the misery of creationism. It was payback time when I dragged Tatiana to the Rotunda—to see the William Andrew Mackay murals. There, on the Rotunda's southern wall, is my personal favorite, the mural celebrating the Treaty of Portsmouth between Russia and Japan, facilitated by the US through Teddy Roosevelt's personal involvement. I showed Tatiana a small miracle of cultural history: written beneath the portraits of three members of the Russian delegation are the names "Witte, Korostovets, Nabokov." In the museum's brochure, Konstantin Nabokov, distinguished Russian diplomat and the uncle of the future author of *Ada, or Ardor*, is mistakenly identified as Vladimir Nabokov, who was five and a half when the Treaty of Portsmouth was signed in Kittery, Maine.

At 6 p.m., we met Sasha and Deena at an Italian restaurant across the street from Lincoln Center. A whole block on Columbus Avenue had been ripped up, and sidewalk tables looked like newcomers' sparkling crowns thrust into the old jaws of scaffolding. We rushed through dinner, without having enough time to catch up.

"Guys, just come with us," I offered again. "I'll get you in without tickets. Come now, Sasha. So you sued their sponsor, but it's over now. Did you lose?"

"No, just about ended where we started," Sasha replied, woe in his voice.

"Who is this guy anyway?" I asked.

"He would describe himself as a businessman and a patron of the arts ... Forget it. Why don't we order more wine," Sasha proposed.

"You want me to fall asleep at the reading?"

Deena asked for another glass of prosecco (a drink that makes me think of prosecution), Sasha helped us flag down a cab, and ten minutes later Tatiana and I were walking past a small crowd of smoking old poets and their admirers as we entered the building of a historic synagogue on East 65th Street.

By the time we came inside, most of the pews in the smaller sanctuary, where the anthology launch and reading were to take place, were filled—save for the first two rows, reserved, as I surmised, for the readers and their families. I immediately fell into the hands of a reporter for a Russian TV station, a woman my age whom I'd met soon after coming to America. Tatiana waited patiently as I waxed sentimental about the "heritage of Russian Jews" in America, something my daughter had heard many times. We finally sat in the second row on the aisle. To our right there was an empty seat with an untouched "reserved" sign, and to the right of the empty seat, lying flat on the cushion, was a large oblong purse with a heavy chain for a strap.

It was then I saw my old friend Yakov Shteynberg, a Russian translator of modern American poets, especially Pound and Eliot. Yakov was slowly moving down the crowded aisle.

"Yakov, over here," I called out, waving and pointing to the vacant seat to our right.

He sat down next to me and started sifting through the contents of his cognac-colored leather bag, until he finally fished out a slim volume of poetry, published in Minsk, and proceeded to inscribe it to Tatiana and me.

Suddenly, a man of about sixty hovered over Yakov. His face was pallid; his hair, dyed ashen brown, was coiffed with such perfection that it almost didn't move with the rest of the man's head. He wore a tight-fitting ventless sport coat with the color pattern known in Russian as "sparks." The oversized round face of his wristwatch showed its diamonds from beneath the stiff cuff of his cream-colored shirt. Sitting next to Yakov was a lady of about fifty, her lips pursed and her bangs slanted à la secretary of a labor union at a piano factory someplace in provincial Russia, from which she may or may not have emigrated years ago. The lady nervously fingered her purse with a mother-of-pearl clasp.

"Why are you sitting in our seat?" the man with the expensive watch sternly asked my friend Yakov.

"I'm a participant of the reading," Yakov softly answered.

"What participant? No-no-no," the man said, and the "no-no-no" part came out in formidable English. "Can't you see these are our seats."

Yakov didn't engage him, but instead simply got up and moved to a seat on the other side of the aisle. From the new seat he waved to me, as if saying "it isn't worth the fuss." But I didn't take heed.

"Why were you so rude to my friend?" I asked, turning to the coiffed man and his lady companion. "He happens to be a wonderful writer. And he's reading today. It was I who asked him to take the empty seat next to me."

"And you, what exactly are you doing here?" the gentleman asked me.

"I'm an avenger of insulted poets," I replied. "And you?"

"I'm the sponsor," the gentleman demurred, lowering his gaze.

Throughout the evening, the "sponsor" and his lady companion kept staring at Tatiana, who listened with one ear while also watching silenced YouTube on her smartphone. I could tell they really wanted to reprimand my daughter but held back.

At the conclusion of the reading, as Tatiana and I made our way toward the long tables with viands and drinks arranged in the synagogue lobby, we came face to face with the publisher Levkov, formerly of Vilnius, later of New York by way of Tel Aviv. One of Levkov's claims to fame was the publication of Kurt Vonnegut in Russian translation.

"She'll make a great soldier for Israel," Levkov greeted me and complimented my daughter. "Do you even know whom you clashed with at the reading?" he asked.

"No idea," I answered sincerely.

"That's Misha the Wolf, the biggest funeral director in all of Russian New York."

"No way? That Wolf? I remember his ads in *New Russian Word*. "A catalog of coffins ..."

"That's right," Levkov nodded. "A very big catalog. Back when you immigrated, he only had one funeral parlor, and now he owns five. In Queens, in the Bronx, two in Brooklyn, and one on Long Island."

"A whole wolf's lair," I tried to make a joke.

Tatiana and I eventually pushed our way to *vodochka* and red caviar (for me) and Coke and eclairs (for her), talked to several other participants of the launch, and left without saying goodbye to the organizers.

It was almost 10 p.m. Our taxi crossed Central Park and turned onto Columbus Avenue.

"Look, papa, Sasha and Deena are still there at the restaurant," my observant daughter pointed out as she looked out the window.

They were indeed still sitting at our table, more than four hours later. Lucky hedonists, I thought as I snapped a photo of the nighttime sidewalk scene with Sasha and Deena hidden in plain view. And I immediately texted the photo to Sasha with the note: "Password: Funeral of the Arts."

Sasha immediately texted back: "Join us?"

"I wish I could, *brat* (which in Russian means 'brother')," I replied. "It's past Tatiana's bedtime."

Sasha texted again: "Sorry we couldn't catch up properly. Now you understand why I didn't want to run into this funeral artist again. Glad we're still on the same wavelength."

And that's how I was convinced, yet again, that art and death are inextricably connected, especially when morticians serve as art sponsors.

After that visit to New York, I started getting emails with promotional offers from Wolk Memorial Chapels. I would read some of them, out of curiosity, and delete others without opening them. One day, a handsome envelope arrived in my university mailbox. It contained a stylish brochure and a personal letter on the firm's stationery. Aside from complimenting my recent book of immigrant novellas, Mikhail Wolk was writing to "draw your attention to our new plan of purchasing burial plots at a cemetery where many of our former compatriots have been laid to rest—artists, writers, musicians." Wolk Memorial Chapels, it continued, "offers cultural figures like you a 30% discount for prepaying the funeral arrangements."

My heart first soared, then grew heavy. As I reread the offer, I couldn't stop thinking of life's vagaries and of the vanity of philanthropists. "Finally," I was thinking. "Finally I've earned my place in the Russian-American necropolis."

All I had to do now was retire from college teaching, move to New York, and die a happy immigrant.

In the Net of Composer N.

Pentiti, cangia vita,
è l'ultimo momento!

—Mozart, *Don Giovanni,*
libretto by Lorenzo Da Ponte

The winter of 1978 was the last time I tasted of the forbidden fruit that Soviet golden youth consumed with habitual indifference. We were spending the winter holiday at Maleyevka, the Writers' Home of Creativity outside Moscow. My parents had entered the path of emigration. My mom had already said goodbye to her beloved job as a professor of business English and interpreter. My father, too, had to bid adieu to the Research Institute of Microbiology, where he had worked since the mid-1960s. My parents had placed their Soviet careers, quite successful for Jews who weren't party members, on the execution block, except that instead of permission to leave, refusenikdom awaited us. For my father, that winter vacation at Maleyevka was also a farewell to his life as a Soviet writer. His official punishment just for the "attempt at exodus" (my father's words) would be not only banishment from academic life but also expulsion from the Union of Soviet Writers, the derailment of three books, and public ostracism. But back then, as a twelve-year-old, I couldn't imagine that my parents ever made mistakes. Nor could we imagine that a year later the Soviet troops would invade Afghanistan as the rule of corpses propelled the USSR into its own unravelling. How could we possibly foresee that I would celebrate my Bar Mitzvah not in the Holy Land but in a Moscow shrouded with summertime poplar snow? In a certain causal sense, the events I describe below had not much to do with the political and personal backdrop of my teenage years, and yet without this backdrop I wouldn't have become the witness and observer typing these lines on a chilly afternoon on May 9, the Day of Victory over Nazi Germany.

The daily routine at the Writers' Home of Creativity, situated at the former estate of the publisher Vykol Lavrov, looked like this: an abundant breakfast heavy on pastries and farmer's cheese, creative time, strolls around the nearby wintry forests and fields, lunch with alcohol, rest, some more creative time, finally billiards and supper with abundant drinking that sometimes continued into the late hours. Writers' spouses and writers' scions spent their entire days in various social amusements. Two groups could be distinguished among the "young generation": boys and girls my age, still innocent but already beginning to don the air of sophistication, and the true golden youth, university students who acted as though the privileges they enjoyed were hereditary, endless, and limitless. Most outrageously behaved was the son of the poet Rimma Kazakova. This young man, who would subsequently become known for his psychedelic fiction, wandered the halls of the old manor house and tried to glue himself to every writer's teenage daughter or granddaughter.

Due to a strange concurrence of circumstances, the core of the group of kids that I was running with during that winter holiday was composed not of the children but rather of the grandchildren of Soviet writers. Our intellectual leader was a boy by the name of Sasha Taratuta, whose Paris-born elderly grandmother, critic and memoirist, was best known for her work on Ethel Lilian Voynich, author of *The Gadfly*, a late Victorian novel about a radicalized English Catholic in *Risorgimento*-era Italy. Voinich's book enjoyed cult status in Soviet Russia and the People's Republic of China. On the day we met, Sasha took me aside and asked, his bright voice lowered to a conspiratorial whisper:

"Have you heard of Composer N.?

"No, I haven't," I answered sincerely.

"What's wrong with you? My grandmother told me all about him. An aristocrat. Emigrated. Went to Cambridge University. Lived in America. Died in Switzerland. A genius!"

Another memorable character in our midst was Mitya Sidorov, swarthy, velvet-eyed, his Ashkenazi origins barely concealed by his father's simple Russian last name. Grandson of Semyon Indursky, editor of *Evening Moscow*, Mitya assigned himself the role of a jejune Don Juan. But I took the most liking to Valyusha Tolstosumova, a classic Moscow young lady with a theatrical voice, amethyst eyes red-streaked from exultation or sorrow, and eyelashes long and gorgeous like wondrous moths pressed to the night sky of Crimea. I liked her very much and did not know what to do about it.

When we first met, I asked Valyusha: "Who's the writer in your family?"

Valyusha pursed her lips and replied: "My grandmother."

"And what exactly did she write?" I continued with the interrogation.

"She apprehended Hitler's teeth," Valyusha replied in a voice that suggested I had inadvertently raised my hand at something sacred.

At the time, in part under the influence of Odessan thieves' songs but also in anticipation of parting with all the lies and gibberish of our Brezhnevite youth, I deliberately put on the persona of a rough street kid, atypical of the young boys from the families of the intelligentsia.

"Yeah, right, Hitler's teeth. Better yet say she found Martin Bormann's liver in Brazil," I mocked Valyusha Tolstosumova's words.

The grandson of the leading Soviet expert on *The Gadfly* gave me a disapproving look.

"You might consider expressing yourself more tactfully," he said.

Had the regular kids with whom I played soccer and hockey in the back yard of our Moscow apartment building heard Sasha Taratuta's words, they would have sentenced him to eternal damnation.

Valyusha shuddered, as if from a gust of cold wind, but said nothing.

In the meantime, the winter break rolled down the icy riverbanks toward the New Year. Sometimes after breakfast, our little group would go cross-country skiing or sledding, although we preferred indoor games. Those included sitting in the deep divans of the main building's spacious living room or playing at billiards when the tables weren't occupied by the proud makers of Soviet literature. In the evening, we amused ourselves with more or less the same activities as did the regular Soviet kids our age—cards, spin the bottle (known in Soviet-speak as "kiss-meow"). Sometimes, if we could find a vacant private space in a remote building, strip poker would become the game of choice.

Besides the girls and boys from literary families, a gang of local village kids would periodically descend upon the halls of Maleyevka. For the most part, they were the children of the dining-hall servers, maids, and cleaning ladies employed to wait on the writers and their families. It was considered a form of higher equalitarianism (or was it reverse snobbism?) not to kick these guttersnipes out of the building, and so there were times when the village kids and our clean-cut bunch would come together. I must admit that the writers' descendants were a little afraid of the "villagers," whereas the vacationing writers, even those of peasant stock, regarded them as a necessary evil. My father, who had descended from generations of Litvak rabbis and Podolian millers— and had spent three wartime years in a remote village in the Urals—loved the peasant children with his heart and raised me in the spirit of respect for the ordinary working people.

I mention this became my upbringing would play a part in the early stages of this story.

A boisterous kid with gaps between his front teeth was the boss of the gang of villagers. His name was Grigory, but he went by "Grishutka." He had very pale blue eyes, wheaten curls, and a fearless grin. Grishutka always held a match in his teeth, and now and then he would roll it out on the top of his tongue. The crest of a wave thus plays with a log ripped away from a raft. Having seen many authors and author's family members over the thirteen years of his life, Grishutka considered himself a connoisseur of literature and took a lively interest in the origins of the writers' children and grandchildren. When we first met, he was conducting an interrogation of the boys and girls who were my daily companions during that winter vacation. He had definitely heard of *The Gadfly* but not about the elderly lady who had had tea with the Irish-born author of the novel. He had known Valyusha Tolstosumova's grandmother—the one who had apprehended Hitler's teeth—from early childhood and seemed to have a soft spot for Valyusha.

"And who's your writer?" Grishutka asked me.

"My dad," I replied. "What's it to you?"

"I keep score," Grishutka chuckled. "Come on, give me the name."

"Petrov," I answered. Back in the late 1950s, following the suggestion of the famous poet Boris Slutsky, my father had taken the penname "David Petrov," based on the Russified first name of his father—my grandfather—Pyotr (Peysakh)

Shrayer. After we became refuseniks and he was banished, my father revived our family name and started signing his works "David Shrayer-Petrov."

"Ah, Petrov," Grishutka nodded with approval. "I know the name." (Petrov, roughly "Mr. Stone or Mr. Peters," is among the most common Russian last names.)

On this basis we became temporary pals.

A couple of times the villagers and the writers' kids even organized joint pranks—turned on the fire extinguisher during a movie screening or hid all the billiard balls in a big trash can—but the divide between us remained huge. The arrival of a new character shifted the dynamics. The new arrival was a myopic, stooped teenage boy with pouty lips and an aristocratic nose. Sounds of decadence and cadences of talent were intertwined in his demeanor. He didn't exactly enter our circle yet elected to stay on the fringes and silently witness our games and mischiefs. When I reconstruct the sequence of events that occurred during my last vacation as a Soviet writer's son, I cannot but recognize a causal link between the appearance of this new character and the subsequent public expulsion of the village urchins. This is what I think happened.

In the hollow after-lunch hour, six or seven of us, writers' children and grandchildren, were hanging out in the billiard room. Suddenly, a flock of village boys rolled out emerged from some place in the underbelly of the main building.

"Well, intelligentsia, wanna shoot some pool?" Grishutka addressed us.

The grandson of the editor of *Evening Moscow* reached out for a pool cue but then Grishutka noticed the new boy and changed his mind.

"Hey new kid, what's your name?" Grishutka accosted him.

The "new kid," who was sitting on the edge of a leather divan, notebook in hand, barely acknowledged Grishutka and spoke in a very soft voice: "Andryusha."

"Well sissy, who's your writer?"

"My grandfather," Andryusha said, still softly.

"And who is your grandfather?" Grishutka wouldn't let go.

The village kids made a circle around us, writers' heirs.

"He is a Formalist. Member of the Academy," Andryusha replied, contempt in his voice.

"Formalist? What's that? Some sort of a playwright?" Grishutka asked, turning the match over on his tongue.

"No, it's a school of literary criticism."

"Wow, that's deep," Grishutka commented. Grinning, he turned to the other village kids. "Do you have a last name, literary critic?" he asked.

"Collaborants," Andryusha replied, his voice devoid of hope.

"Labo'rats?" Grishutka chortled, very pleased with himself. The other village boys joined in. "What are you? Kebab? Armo?"

Andryusha Collaborants lowered his gaze and said nothing in return. I noticed that Valyusha Tolstosumova blushed, her eyes tearing up. The other writers' kids pretended that they didn't hear the ethnic slurs.

"Grishutka, leave him alone," I said.

"Petrov, what's it to you?" Grishutka turned his face to me and spread his shoulders, as though getting ready for a fight. "You aren't his relative, are you?"

"I could be if I wanted to," I replied. "Now get lost, Grishutka, before I've put your face where your ass is."

We both hit each other simultaneously. I struck him on his nose, just as my father, a former boxer, had instructed me. Grishutka hit me on the upper lip. We latched onto each other and rolled down the carpet, its thick pelt imprinted with the footsteps of the classics of socialist realism. When they finally pulled us apart, Grishutka had a bloody nose, I—a bloody lip.

"Let's get the hell out of here," Grishutka ordered his gang. "Watch out, Petrov," he barked at me, and they sped out.

Valyusha Tolstosumova ran to the washroom and brought a page of the *Literary Gazette*, which she had skillfully folded into a strip and run under cold water to make a lead compress.

"Press it to your lip and hold," she said.

In the evening, my lip bruised and swollen, I told my parents what had transpired.

"His grandfather was a Formalist? Who could this be? Eikhenbaum? No. Tynyanov? No. And most definitely not Shklovsky," said my father.

Viktor Shklovsky, the half-Jewish, quarter-German, and quarter-Latvian survivor of the great early Soviet experiment in the arts, had twice been my father's recommender for the Union of Soviet Writers.

"This Andryusha kid has his father's last name," I explained. "And the famous grandfather is on the mother's side."

"What kind of an unusual last name is it?" asked my mother, who was trained as a philologist. "Coll-ab-or-rants?"

My father strictly forbade me to complain. "You fight, you make up. Not a big deal," he said. "We don't have snitches in our family."

Following the conflict with Grishutka, the village kids stopped showing up at the House of Creativity. The grandson of the country's leading interpreter of *The Gadfly* told us that he knows "for certain" that the head administrator of Maleyevka "got a call" from Moscow.

Andryusha stopped showing his face in the divan room and billiard room, and Valyusha also dropped out of our daily activities.

After New Year's my parents and I returned to Moscow, and I never again visited Maleyevka or socialized with the descendants of Soviet writers.

We were refuseniks for eight and a half years and emigrated only in early June 1987. In the spring of 1993, a US passport warming my heart, I was finally able to go back to Russia. After that time—and until the start of the COVID-19 pandemic—I went there almost every year. Since graduate school, one of the main objects of my research was Composer N., the great Russian and American modernist and butterfly expert, he of whom I had first heard as a twelve-year-old at the writers' resort outside Moscow.

In the summer of 1998, I found myself in the ancestral mansion of Composer N. on Bolshaya Morskaya Street in St. Petersburg, where a museum had opened not long before that. It's just a couple of blocks from St. Isaac's Cathedral, one of the city's most beautiful spots. The museum occupied only the first floor of the house where Composer N. had spent his pre-Revolutionary childhood. The second and third floors were now being used by a music school and a weekly newspaper. The first director of the Museum of Composer N. was a stylish gentleman who earned himself the sobriquet "Director Snark." He sported a floral tie given to him by the only son of Composer N., an opera singer who lived in Milan. Drop by drop, small bit by small bit, Director Snark put together the museum's collection—first editions and some manuscripts, trays with pinned butterflies, the composer's tweed coat, pince-nez, and amber cigarette holder, family photos, the gramophone that once belonged to Composer N.'s mother. Director Snark also founded the international summer festivals, which happened at the peak of white nights. In the late 1990s, when hope of Russia's democratic future still hung in the air, the summer festivals were attended not only by the students, performers, and interpreters of Composer N. but also by his émigré relatives, among whom stood out one mellifluous baron with a hyphenated German name, a perfectly straight back, and a residence in a toy principality tucked away on the border of Austria and Switzerland.

After Director Snark came a young woman with an Edgar Allan Poe–indebted last name who spoke a rich, beautiful, slightly old-fashioned Russian. She wanted very much for the House of Composer N. to become a center of free and independent culture—a tall order for Russia. But she ended up moving to the US to attend graduate school, and her position went to another museum director, of whom I know precious little. By now we've nearly restored the time frame leading up to the central events of this story.

In the early 2000s, the museum became the object of attempted hostile takeovers. In the end, the takeovers did not succeed, although they all but destroyed the museum's well-being and liquidity. Culturologists campaigned to turn the House of Composer N. into a salon for St. Petersburg intelligentsia. It was rumored that a powerful oligarch sought to expel the newspaper, the music school, and the museum all at once so as to turn the granite-laid mansion into a private residence. I also heard that somewhere in the upper echelons of the Russian government a fight over the museum's status was unfolding: municipal, regional, or national. All sorts of rumors swirled around the museum, and I would periodically learn them from St. Petersburg colleagues and acquaintances while both believing and refusing to believe these accounts.

And then, in the early spring of 2003, I got a Skype call from Venya Belotserkovsky. A notable St. Petersburg personality, Venya was a roving encyclopedia of all things, a survivor of the siege, a hero of Saigon (not the Vietnamese city but the legendary Leningrad café where the literati used to hang out), and the first Russian bibliographer of Composer N. Venya had some ancient version of Skype on his prehistoric computer, and one could only talk by taking turns, but not simultaneously.

"I have two grand pieces of news," Venya screamed. "Which one do you want first?"

"Venya, how about the one that will take less time to explain," I replied.

"You Americans, always in a rush ... Fine, listen to this. The museum is about to become part of St. Petersburg University—especially fortunate since our beloved composer had attended lectures there prior to fleeing Russia. Do you get it?"

"Not completely," I admitted.

"All of you become thick in your America," Venya said.

"It's the calories," I acknowledged. "So what does all this mean for the museum?"

"This all means that the museum is now under the wing of the nation's second-best university. And the university president is an educated and cultured person. He adores Composer N. *Capeesh?*"

"Venya, I have little faith in cultured state officials. But if you say so, I'm glad."

"That's not all of it. You know who the new director is?"

"Of course I don't!"

"Our new director, Valyusha Tolstosumova, wrote her PhD thesis on Composer N.'s life in exile. She's wonderful, smart. And she's all ours. Her *grandmaman*—your father surely must have known her—is the one who apprehended Hitler's body in 1945. Imagine what kind of a family our Valyusha comes from!"

Venya finished his tirade.

"Venya, I believe I met her as a kid. Not the grandmother but Valyusha herself."

"Even better. You'll be in the core of our museum's friends and benefactors," Venya concluded. "We're just starting to plan the summer festival. We need you."

Thus I became a member of the organizing committee of the International Festival of Composer N. And in the summer of 2003, I came to the museum on Bolshaya Morskaya and saw Valyusha again—after twenty-five years. On that Thursday morning during the first week of July, I walked on Malaya Morskaya Street toward St. Isaac's Square, pressed my hand to the memorial plaque on the wall of the hotel where poet Esenin either took his life or was murdered by Russia's secret police in 1925, and thence, across the landscaped garden, ran toward the corner of Bolshaya Morskaya. From there it's just a birdcherry pit's throw to the museum.

The participants and performers were starting to arrive for the opening of the festival. I entered and stopped at the threshold of the reception hall with the familiar, handsome monograms on the ornate ceiling. I saw a slender woman clad in a dress made of something musliny and airy, suede pumps on her feet. Of the original thirteen-year-old Valyusha, whom I remembered from Maleyevka in 1978, only long mothlike eyelashes had survived. That and her voice of remarkable purity and clarity.

In the evening, following the opening day of the festival program, Valyusha and I circled the city as it slowly tried on the last, luminous cloaks of white nights. We ended up eating at a little place called "Idiot"—named after Dostoevsky's novel.

"Valyusha, do tell," I went on prying. "You, a Muscovite, living in Petersburg?"

"Long story, really. I married way early. He was from Leningrad. And then ... then Composer N. You know how it is. A love. Then graduate school, research. And so I stayed here. Sounds crazy, doesn't it? Gradually I got used to it, even became attached to this city. But I miss Moscow all the time."

"My mom also missed Moscow," I said. "And so mom and dad went back after two years here. That's how I was born. Not in Leningrad but in Moscow." And then, as if casually, I asked: "And your husband, what's his story?"

"Former husband. We parted. Five years it's been. He's living in Tel Aviv."

"A familiar story," I said, pulling on my dark beer with a caraway nose. "Did you know that nearly half of that Maleyevka bunch of writers' kids has emigrated. I mainly know this from Facebook. Some are living in New York, others in Berlin, others yet in London ..."

Valyusha didn't say anything. A bluish haze descended on the city that Composer N. never could forget even after sixty years without.

"You know what, Valyusha," I blurted out. "If I weren't married—happily married—I would hit on you."

Valyusha lowered her head just so, and a golden braid of her hair slid down her cheek and fell into her glass of Georgian white wine.

"I thought you liked a different kind of girl. Tobogan. Tennis. Travel ...," said Valyusha all the while kneading her gray linen napkin.

"Whereas I thought you liked nerdy, high-strung boys. Of the sort that can't ski but have read *Coriolanus* ..."

Ten years went by since my reunion with Valyusha. Every summer I would travel to Russia and return to the house of Composer N. for the summer festivals. A remarkable group of younger colleagues worked there alongside Valyusha. These Russian boys and girls, having come of age in the early post-Soviet years, were quite different from my generation, formed and warped during the Brezhnev years. These young people had different brains, different sensibilities. With their enthusiasm, Valyusha had managed to turn the House of Composer N. into a first-rate museum with a fine library of print editions, an archive of its own, and a collection of personal artifacts that had belonged to Composer N. and his family members.

Valyusha and I enjoyed the kind of collegial commerce that sometimes connects people who knew each other as children. She would trust me with delicate tasks—not just the oversight of the festival program but interpersonal matters, such as convincing a brilliant but intolerable Texas academic to participate or else to mediate in the conflict of two veterans of our festivals, opera historian M. and musicologist W. One thing Valyusha and I didn't delve into was family life. She knew from Facebook that my wife had become a full professor of medicine and our daughters had started middle school; I knew that her son from the first marriage had entered university. But of marriage and matrimony we spoke not. It just happened this way.

In November of 2013, I flew to Moscow to participate in a book fair. I was doing an event for a new book. And I had also been invited to participate in the launch of a special literary issue of the Moscow magazine *Snob*, to which I had contributed a Russian version of my short story "A Sunday Walk to the Arboretum."

In those days the book fair, known as Non/fiction, was held at the Krymsky Val exhibition hall. During the pre-sunset hour, I walked from Culture Park metro station in order to photograph the famous bridge under which the *innamorati* kiss in the opening shots of *The Cranes Are Flying*. The same spot appears later in the film, already after Aleksey Batalov's character has been sent to the war front to fight the German invaders. Aleksey Shvorin's character now waits for the young Tatiana Samoilova, who plays Veronika and would later play Anna Karenina.

I photographed the bridge and walked to the exhibition hall. I received my badge and located the auditorium assigned for the *Snob* reading. Right next to it there was a cafeteria and a lounge, and right there in line to get my coffee and eclair I ran into Valyusha Tolstosumova. She was wearing a zigzagy Missoni dress and high-heeled shoes of dark blue suede. Only her fashionably messy hair and the moths of her eyelashes were the same.

"Valyusha, are you reading?" I asked, dropping my smartphone onto the counter. "Following in your grandmother's steps?"

"Of course not," Valyusha replied as we brush-kissed on the cheek. "Just here to listen. And this evening I'm coming to your book event."

Valyusha turned in the direction of divans and low tables piled up with paper plates and cups and waved to somebody."

"Do you remember Andryusha?" she asked in her bell jar voice.

This sometimes happens in a dream: from a maelstrom of the past a dead body floats up, a dead body of a person you haven't seen in over half a lifetime, and pulls up a chain of needless memories.

"Of course I remember," I replied while simultaneously replaying in my head the episode with Grishutka, the fight, and the banishment of village kids from the Writers' House of Creativity at Maleyevka.

Together we approached the low coffee table where Andryusha Collaborants was sitting. Valyusha introduced— or rather, reintroduced—us. She looked at Andryusha adoringly. He and I exchanged a few noncommittal phrases—about the years "flying posthaste," the magazine that feels "like a good American quarterly," and also about "living life in both capitals."

A little later, during the reading, when Andryusha came up to the microphone, I managed to catch a good look of him. Years hadn't done much to the twelve-year-old grandson of the famous Formalist scholar and Member of the Soviet Academy, the youth who used to sit with a slender notebook in hand, observing the other kids' fun and games. The thin-legged boyish man who stood at the microphone was dressed in an elegantly tailored, checkered coat and narrow blue jeans. A birthmark below his left cheekbone, a fleshy nose, and large pouted lips stood out on his pale waxen face. No wonder the kids at Maleyevka used to call him "platypus." The adult Andryusha had long, oily hair. The thick lenses of his small rimless glasses distorted the shape of his eyes. The eyes dashed to and fro, forming a wondrous stroboscopic pattern. For some reason I also remembered the thin mother-of-pearl fingers of Andryusha Collaborants, the sharp cleft of his chin, and the simultaneous expression of languor and laceration that punctuated the lines of prose he delivered.

Written in first person and chockfull of allusions to sadomasochism and sexual domination, the excerpt from his new novel described discord between two Russian lovers come to London for two weeks. The hero and heroine spend most of the day strolling through the autumnal Regents Park until they find themselves in Camden Town. The hero, visibly drawn from his creator, constantly speaks about missing Russia. The heroine outwardly resembles Valyusha, except the author has taken away her mild demeanor and natural talent for self-sacrifice, having turned her into a wretched creature that teases and torments the hero. The entire excerpt communicates a presentiment of breaking up, except it's not the vile heroine but the suffering hero who does the dirty work. And he doesn't just break up but cheats on her with a streetwalker from a small Balkan country.

I left the reading in low spirits. How was it possible that Valyusha, the wonderful, decent, honest Valyusha, had joined her life with such a creep? This is what I was thinking as I walked down Ostozhenka Street in the direction of the Pushkin Museum of Art and the monument to the anarchist Prince Kropotkin.

Later, after I got back home to Boston, I made inquiries and found out a few things. To wit: Valyusha Tolstosumova was the third wife of Andryusha Collaborants. That is, no longer Andryusha but Professor Andrey Yurievich Collaborants, author of many novels and stories but also various publications on modern culture, in which he managed to touch on topics not quite accepted in Russia—now queerness in music and literature, now totalitarian art. And yet he also stuck to the party line and supported Russia's annexation of Crimea. Having come across a long interview on YouTube, I was struck by the amplitude of his ramblingly articulate comments, ranging from his grandfather and other Russian Formalists to the destiny of Sergey Prokofiev, but also not failing to mention how St. Petersburg was "fortunate to have such a high benefactor in the Kremlin …"

Two more years slid by. The museum at Bolshaya Morskaya Street was slowly dying. The signs of an imminent crisis were already becoming evident in the summer of 2017. Suddenly there were fewer foreign visitors and participants, as though they sensed the alarm and refused to attend. The reception hall of the House of Composer N. now teemed with bureaucrats from a newly instituted university office with a sinister name, and these men and women had first names and patronymics taken from the smelly trunks of Soviet history: Vladlen Nikitich (from Vladimir Lenin and Nikita Khrushchev), Octyabrina Iosifovna (from October Revolution and Iosif Stalin) and so forth. Where did these petty monsters come from? They would show up at the opening events of the festival, sit in the back row, jot something down in their notebooks, then noisily get up and leave in the middle of a presentation. Valyusha had also changed. She would speak cursively about the affairs of the museum, waving off queries. Many years of living in the US had taught me not to pester people with personal questions, respecting the distance the others choose for their own comfort. I thought: If she doesn't want to engage, this means she is just unable to do it, physically or emotionally. And I accepted the new terms.

Was I even surprised when, in late December 2017, I got a Skype call from Venya Belotserkovsky? He had aged but hadn't lost his youthful passion.

"Things are bad, good pal. There's a new president at the university."

"Did they get rid of the cultured one?" I couldn't help asking.

"No time to make jokes," Venya said scornfully. "Our museum's in jeopardy."

"Venya, how can I help?"

"I don't know yet. The museum is being audited. They have turned everything upside down. Valyusha's going to have a nervous breakdown. We need to save her, do you understand?"

Reluctantly, I did some research of my own. The new university president, known for his choleric temperament and dictatorial style, was a Putin appointee and intended to run the university in the style of a military settlement. He was surrounding himself with a retinue of lackeys, of whom he demanded unconditional execution of his will. It didn't exactly surprise me that Andryusha Collaborants was appointed the new chair of cultural studies. Russia's increasingly repressive regime needed such scions of famous intellectuals, such refined, openly vulnerable marionettes, writers of the slightly perverse but politically loyalist fictions. Why? In order to create the illusion of a free culture. But how is any of this compatible with Valyusha? She, too, I had no doubt of it, could see through it. How, then?

Winter sooty clouds had gathered over the House of Composer N. In the spring of 2018, one by one, the younger museum workers left—the idealistic Russian boys and girls who had given their beloved museum ten years of their lives. They were now in their early thirties, not yet hopeless cynics but no longer buoyant with hope for Russia's future. First Margarita Bulganinova, then Seryozha Danilov. Their replacements, sent to the House of Composer N. from the university office of surveillance and control, were foppish young men in tight grey suits and young ladies with braided hair and very Russian names. Valyusha Tolstosumova was now all alone ...

At the end of April, Valyusha called my office number. This was highly irregular.

"Valyusha, you? Please hold on a sec, a student's just leaving ..."

Having seen my advisee out the door, I took a gulp of cold tea with lemon and pressed the receiver to my temple.

"Valyusha, is everything ok?"

"I'm sorry to call like that...."

I could hear she was choking on words.

"What, Valyusha, just say it!"

"They fired me."

"How? Those reptiles."

"Andrey has been appointed the new museum director."

"Which Andrey?" I asked, unable to accept the obvious.

"My Andrey. I mean he's no longer mine. I left him. I just can't take it any more ..."

"Valyusha, so sorry. I don't know what to say."

"There's nothing to say. Just please don't judge me, that's all I ask."

From various sources, I had pieced together the unraveling at the former House of Composer N. Andryusha Collaborants had initially developed a frenzied schedule of activities. Most of the museum's permanent display was removed, crated, and stored in a remote depository. The museum became a venue for trendy events, and the new director populated his Noah's Ark of culture not only with writers known for their criticism of the regime, and not just commercially successful, venal littérateurs and performing artists, but also so-called "patriots"—Ahlabustin, Prilepin. Collaborants even invited A. Prokhanov, leader of the so-called Red-Browns, to the May Artfest. There was nothing surprising in the fact that various dubious characters were eager to perform at the former House of Composer N. It's harder to explain why decent people with reputations agreed to accept Collaborants's invitations. The public in St. Petersburg split into those who boycotted the museum and those who refused to do so. In some sense the whole fight may have seemed like a naval battle in a pitcher of water. And yet those of us who had long been involved with the museum and had been supporters of Valyusha Tolstosumova couldn't bring ourselves to do business with the new director of the museum. It was decided—for the first time since the founding of the museum—to move the summer festival to a different venue.

It had been a difficult decision. Luckily, the Academy Institute of Russian Culture agreed to shelter our festival in its historic auditorium under a gilded dome. This building on Makarova Embankment was perfectly suited for what we now called the Composer N. Summer Festival. How odd that we hadn't thought of it previously! A two-day program had already been put together, evening public events, concerts, and panels had been assembled when, just a week prior to the opening, our hosts at the Institute of Russian Culture hinted that it would probably be a good idea to invite Professor

Collaborants to say a few words at the opening ceremony. He was, after all, the director of the only house-museum of the great Composer N., and it would be unseemly to snub him. The majority of the core members of the organizing committee were in favor of avoiding a scandal. Only Venya Belotserkovsky was furious and kept sending us collective, wrathful emails about conformism and the "price of complacency." Venya was against it, the others—for it. And Valyusha Tolstosumova said nothing. Reluctantly we agreed to invite Andryusha Collaborants. Six short days and six long white nights remained before the opening of the festival.

I am embroidering the background with so many details so as to emphasize that none of us festival organizers had any inkling that something unimaginable would happen at the opening. Now picture a July morning, the packed auditorium with wall portraits of Russian enlighteners and Pushkin's bronze statuette. Feel the wet wind from the Neva pouring in through the open tops of the tall windows. The director of the Institute of Russian Culture opened the festival, then gave the floor to a lovely ancient lady who had authored biographies of many Russian composers, Scriabin and Stravinsky among them. Finally, Andryusha Collaborants made his way to the podium. He unfolded a sheet with his prepared remarks, glanced over it, and started to speak. At first his lips trembled, but then the little satan of eloquence sprang up and Andryusha spoke fluidly and fluently. His speech was propped up by the same rhetorical device as most of his fictions: people are weak, life is turbulent, authorities are merciful. In a trained fashion, Andryusha circled the auditorium with his right hand and delivered this polished sentence:

"We're all butterflies in his splendid collection."

At this point the fearless Venya Belotserkovsky jumped up from his chair.

"No, Collaborants, you are not a butterfly," Venya yelled. "You're a vermin."

For a moment Andryusha turned into the preteen snitch who had refused to go along with our pranks. But then he must have remembered his age and status and protested in his bleating voice:

"But how dare you? I shall submit a formal complaint!"

And then chords of some divine music wafted in. The domed ceiling of the auditorium was either opened or pulled apart, and a hand clasping an immense white butterfly net appeared across a glaring sky. The net was lowered over Andryusha Collaborants. Stealthily, the right hand of Composer N., its monogrammed cufflink furiously sparkling, sliced the air with the bottom of the net, cutting off its victim's escape. Andryusha was fluttering and flapping in the cone of the net, shrieking with endless fear, but it was too late. The hand with the net bent at the elbow and raised itself through the open vault of the auditorium. The whole thing was so mercilessly beautiful that all of those present got up from their seats, turned up their heads, and followed the trajectory of the net carrying away its human booty. It almost appeared that it wasn't the toy museum director in the net of Composer N. but the disappearing tail of a northern comet.

Only Valyusha Tolstosumova dashed to the microphone and screamed in some antiterrestrial voice: "I beg of you, please stop. Take pity on him …"

It was then I understood that despite his betrayal, Valyusha still loved her Collaborants.

The domed ceiling closed. Shaking their stupor, people shuffled their feet and spoke with relief.

This story has three epilogues: the desired, the disposed, and the destined.

Institutional justice, as is well known, triumphs very rarely, and especially so in Russia. In the desired epilogue, the tyrannical university president got transferred from St. Petersburg to assume a ministerial post in Moscow. Valyusha Tolstosumova was restored to her position, and the dedicated associates followed her back to the House of Composer N.

But alas, this hasn't happened (and is unlikely to happen), and a new acting director of the former House of Composer N. has been appointed to replace Collaborants. An employee of the same university office of surveillance and control, she bears the name Elizaveta Vilorievna Podmyshkina. And instead of salvation through art, we must contend with the brutal reality of life. But not all is lost.

At the beginning of December 2018, I drove from Chestnut Hill across the river to meet a colleague for lunch in Cambridge. After lunch at an old burger place in Harvard Square, I decided to walk to the Museum of Comparative Zoology. This was on a sleety day when fall and winter were fighting out one of their last battles. In the early afternoon, the museum was empty save for a retiree couple and a homeless lepidopterologist wearing a Russian winter hat. I stopped in front of a massive wall cabinet containing parts of the collection of butterflies described and classified by Composer N. Looking over my left shoulder, I randomly pulled out first one tray of butterflies, then another. On the fifth or sixth attempt, I located a glass-covered tray with the item I was hoping to find yet didn't quite believe I would.

There, in the middle of the tray, next to a specimen of the Garner Blue that Composer N. had measured and studied up and down and across, from proboscis to abdomen and from forewings to antennae, a little bespectacled man was pinned down to the bottom of the tray. He rested there, like a bather on the surface of a frothy sea, atop a moiré butterfly, she a double-winged American beauty with a stamp of eternity on her ashen wings.

Only One Day in Venice

Oh, agony! that centuries should reap
No mellower harvest! Thirteen hundred years
Of wealth and glory turned to dust and tears...
—Lord Byron

This story began thirty-five years ago and refuses to come to an end ...

In the summer of 1987, my parents and I came to Italy from Moscow by way of Vienna. We waited for our American refugee visas by the shores of the Tyrrhenian Sea in the town of Ladispoli, best known for sharing a train station with Cerveteri, site of the famous *tumuli*—Etruscan burial mounds. At the end of our Italianate summer, my parents and I took a low-budget bus tour of Northern Italy, which brought us first to Florence, then Bologna and San Marino, and finally to Venice. The organizers only allotted one day and one night for Venice, and in my immigrant memory of those twenty-four hours have lasted for an eternity. Not merely eternity, but eternity in a repository of beauty.

But unlocking this story about a Jewish-Russian émigré returning to Venice requires one more silver-plated key, one that has very little to do with emigration and the lives of

exiles. In February of 2017 my wife Karen and our daughters Mira and Tatiana spent three weeks in Italy. On our first day of skiing in the Dolomites, a snowboarder from Berlin lost control and rammed into me at full speed. I won't bore you with the details of where his grandfather had served on the Eastern Front during the war, but I will tell you that I was very, very lucky to have ended up with four broken ribs. It could have all been much worse as Doctor Death had been aiming for my spleen. In any event, I couldn't ski. In the morning I would walk my wife and daughters to the nearest lift at Santa Croce, then return to our mountain resort, drink double espressos, and compose true stories. And I did my darndest to make sure that my loved ones wouldn't develop a guilt complex.

The following summer I entered the sixth decade of my life, and my wife and daughters decided that I deserved a make-up week of skiing in (the former) South Tyrol. Everything had been perfectly conceived, and it's well known that perfect plans augur calamitous complications. We were flying via Paris to Venice. In Venice we would have two days for jetlag therapy and total immersion in splendor. On the morning of our third day in Italy, we were supposed to drive up to the Dolomites. The magnanimous calendar was putting us in Venice on the eve of Christmas, which appeared to us, righteous Judeans, as a particularly alluring prospect.

On 23 December 2017, we arrived at Logan Airport, zipped through security, and boarded a Delta aircraft. The Paris flight was leaving at 7:15 in the evening. Here started our misadventures. First we sat in the plane for a whole hour, waiting for the luggage to be loaded—the cargo loader had gotten stuck due to frost. Our Boeing 767 finally entered the runway, gained speed, and then ... some pebbly sprites started to grate and vibrate somewhere inside the plane, and we came to a halt. The captain announced that there was something wrong with the rudder and we were returning to the terminal. Then came an hour of utter chaos—waiting for technical assistance, taxiing back to the terminal, and finally being allowed to deplane. All the while no instructions were given. My wife, who was born in Philadelphia and grew up in New England, said that the country was "falling apart," and I readily agreed, visualizing in my head the pigeons of San Marco and the gondoliers in woven straw hats with dangling ribbons. Resorting to the entire arsenal of my Russian, Jewish, American—and former Soviet—rhetoric, I convinced a Delta shift manager that it was absolutely essential for my family to be in Europe in the morning, or else universal harmony would be disrupted. She promised us seats on a plane for Amsterdam, but then it turned out that they wouldn't be able to release our checked suitcases from the original plane until they had figured out the source of the malfunction. And without suitcases they couldn't send us off to a different destination (read: destiny). She spoke all of this in a half-whisper, awakening heavy thoughts about the true reason for our flight's delay. I won't describe the next two hours. I'll only say that they had towed the plane away to some hangar so as to perform various tests, and only at 1 in the morning did they announce that the flight would be leaving after all.

We landed at Charles de Gaulle not at 8 in the morning as planned but at 3 o'clock in the afternoon. Picture a plane full of travelers who missed their flights, all channeled into a seething line at the Delta/KLM/Air France service desk. After making our way to the counter, we fell into the hands of a smiley agent by the name of Karim, who immediately assured us that he would be "taking care of everything," including the "little lady" (referring to Tatiana), who looked "*fâchée et fatigué.*" There were no more direct flights to Venice, and so we would be connecting in Rome, and at 10:30 in the evening, G-d willing, we would land in the Lagoon.

"What about our luggage? Our ski boots and all?" Karen and I asked.

"I've already sent your suitcases to Venice," answered the coral-toothed Karim, handing us new boarding passes, meal vouchers, and silver pins with the Delta logo for our daughters (who politely accepted but never did wear the pins).

After that, things began to look up, and the gelato at Fiumicino was genuine, and even the flight to Venice was only delayed by a quarter of an hour. At Marco Polo, we waited in vain for the luggage carousel to return our suitcases. There was only one agent at the lost paradise counter. A middle-aged Venetian lady with a big face peered into her computer and informed us, contempt in her voice, that our luggage had either been sent "to Atlanta or someplace else." Again feeling low on luck, we came out of the terminal. Water taxis weren't running due to heavy fog. It was already 11:30 at night, a deserted airport on Christmas eve. A cab finally pulled up, and the driver agreed to take us as far as Piazzale Roma, and then called a water taxi for us.

The real Venice revealed herself with glimmering lights on the surface of the Grand Canal. The girls cheered up from our night boat ride, and Karen and I also brightened up. At the boat landing of Hotel Saturnia (almost Saturnalia), a monocled night porter was waiting for us. The windows of our two-story suite faced Rio della Vesta. We went to bed at one in the morning. Ahead of us lay an entire day in Venice. Only one day.

The day started and ended in San Marco. Like a brilliant poem or time-perfected work of fiction, Venice was unrecognizably recognizable. Venetian women clad in long tunics still threw themselves into canals from the embankments (*pace* Pasternak). Purple pigeons alighted from under the feet of my beloved K., while a melancholy winged lion lowered his mane over a bronze Gospel folio. Amid this beauty, a Jew nearly forgot that Venice was also the birthplace of the ghetto ... In the end, we never took our daughters to Cannaregio, where Venetian Jews used to wake up, hope in their eyes, and go to sleep, despair in their hearts. With lightness and ease, watermarks left our wallets, imprinting themselves on the golden canals and disappearing beyond the waterline. And of course, we bumped into my literary peer, a Moscow twitterato by the name of Dmitri B., who was sitting in a café with a view of the Piazzetta and of San Giorgio Maggiore farther ahead, a tablet next to an empty cup, sitting there and furiously dispatching yet another declaration of love for Venice.

Having occupied ourselves with a guided tour of the Palace of the Doges, an abundant lunch, and a stroll to Rialto and back, we decided to swing by the hotel and check on our luggage. Gianluca, the porter whom the Russian immigrant in me had nicknamed Ivan Lukitch Portobelov, telephoned the airport and found out that the suitcases had already been located, picked up from the airport, and driven to a transfer point in Mestre, and from there they were supposed to be delivered by boat directly to our hotel. I'm copying the dialogue I jotted down in my travel journal:

"Delivered when?"

"It's Christmas, so it would have to be tomorrow afternoon."

"You're joking, right? Tomorrow morning we're leaving for the mountains. The suitcases have all our ski stuff."

"I'm very sorry, *signore.*"

"You don't look too sorry; otherwise you would be doing something to help."

And thus first in Italian, then in English.

In the evening we had tickets to a holiday Corelli and Vivaldi concert at the Church of San Vidal. Remember *The Four Seasons*? There's this moment in "L'inverno," devastating. In the middle of the Allegro non molto your heart stops for a split second. You know all's lost but not forever ...

When we returned to the hotel, our corpulent suitcases were lined up in front of our suite. All the contents were intact, save for one inexplicable detail. Packed into one of the regained suitcases had been three copies of the second Moscow edition of the Russian translation of my memoir *Waiting for America*, which I had intended to give as gifts to my colleagues—Italian professors of Russian literature. And so imagine, in one of the suitcases, instead of the Russian books, I discovered three copies of *Aspettando America*, the

Italian translation of my book. Three copies with bright greet covers and a bottle of prosecco wrapped with a ribbon just like the ones worn on a gondolier's straw hat.

We immediately uncorked the Italian bubbly, and I took one copy of the book and inscribed it to our Hotel Saturnia—where, as it turned out, Ray Charles used to stay. And so now my book rests in a glass display in the lobby, next to a vase of emerald green Venetian glass and a signed photograph of the blind American jazz player.

Would that we always had such occasions to unburden ourselves of the baggage of the past!

Yelets Women's High School

What was I hoping for, what was I expecting, what portent future life did I envision when I reacted with only a momentary sigh, with only a forlorn recollection to the fleeting phantom of my first love that passed before me?

—Ivan Turgenev

Blood vessels of Russian classical literature saturate this story the way capillaries do the vermillion border of human lips. And yet the American in me is having trouble with a traditional structure: the prologue juts out like the Habsburg jaw, the middle of the story bulges like a hernia, and the finale is missing entirely. Having resigned myself to the idea that life's raw material dictates its own rules of storytelling, I have decided to offer the account of these events exactly as they presented themselves.

It all started in Moscow in late autumn of 1985—the hardest year in our family's post-World War II history. My parents and I had been living as Jewish refuseniks since 1979. In November 1985, the Soviet secret police set in motion a new round of my father's persecution. An ostracized writer and medical scientist, he was being accused of anti-Soviet activities, of spreading what the authorities called "Zionist" literature. Law enforcement officers delivered a summons from the office of the Moscow city attorney ("prosecutor," in Sovietspeak) to our doorstep. My father went into hiding. The terrible stress he was under resulted in a heart attack and hospitalization at Moscow's City Hospital No. 4. Plainclothes agents came to interrogate my father on the intensive care floor. "If you want his death, go ahead," an attending physician told them. The professional thugs wavered. Late at night my mother and I met with a bearded *New York Times* correspondent and passed to him an open letter of protest.

Against the backdrop of my family's tribulations, I continued to attend Moscow University, where I was a sophomore at the School of Soil Science. It was a place I didn't appreciate enough for having given me, a Jew and a son of refusenik activists, a salutary deferral from the military draft at a time when the country was still sending her young lads to slaughter in Afghanistan. I went through a spiral of misadventures in the autumn of 1985, triggered by my own efforts to break away from natural sciences and enter the world of art. A failed attempt to switch to a major in art history nearly resulted in my expulsion from the university. With much difficulty I was able to backpedal to soil science, but my position became more vulnerable and would so remain until late spring of 1987, when the Soviet authorities finally granted us permission to leave ...

Now visualize the first week of January 1986 in Moscow. Just a few days prior, at a New Year celebration with a group of

Soviet youths from the Jewish urban intelligentsia—many of us having known each other since childhood—there was spontaneous talk about the country's new course of "liberalization," of Gorbachev's having finally taken charge of the party, and of the appointment of Yeltsin as Moscow's party boss. One of my pals, a student at the Institute of Oil and Gas (nicknamed "ink-blotter") and a great fan of the Soviet *chansonniers,* whispered in my ear: "I heard on the Voice of America that Yeltsin isn't a retrograde and certainly not an antisemite. And he even plays tennis." Of course he does!

On the first day of the spring semester, as I traversed the yawning vestibule of Moscow University's main tower, I spotted an announcement: "Courses for Directors of the People's Theaters." Below were the address of the university theater and the time of the admission interviews. At the time I hadn't yet learned to differentiate between life's false messages and true signs of destiny. In the evening, as my parents and I gathered for supper, I couldn't stop talking about the announcement.

"Wouldn't it be amazing if they accepted you?" said my mother.

"In the 1960s it used to be a good theater," said my father. "Once I even talked with Rolan Bykov, who was then artistic director."

"What about?"

"A comedy. About the discovery of the smallpox vaccine," my father explained.

"But what could I offer them?" I asked my parents. "My theatrical experience is negligible."

"You had lead parts in school performances," said my mother.

"School performances? It's a joke. *The Prince and the Pauper*? *Passasunder*?" (At Moscow Linguistic University, from which my mother had graduated, students referred to Peter Abrahams's anti-apartheid novel *The Path of Thunder*, shoved down their throats by the Soviet curriculum, as "Passasunder.")

"Don't undersell yourself," my father advised. "Hold on tight to the classics. They'll always be at your side. Conjure up some playwriting device. Propose staging Pushkin. You'll be fine, you'll see."

A wintry evening in the middle of January, my native city of Moscow buried in snow. I walked—ran—from the intersection of the former Gorky Street down Tverskoy Boulevard, then along Herzen Street (now un-renamed Bolshaya

Nikitskaya) all the way down to Manège Square. This was my favorite of Moscow's theatrical and musical routes: past the new stage of the Moscow Arts Theater, then the Theater on Malaya Bronnaya (formerly the State Yiddish Theater), the Mayakovsky Theater, and the Moscow Conservatory of Music (which students of my generation dubbed *konserva*, roughly "canned music"). I reached the dimly lit bottom of Herzen Street, and there it was, the recessed corner building on the right side of the street.

Four people conducted the interviews: Iosif Lopatkin, the theater's artistic director; Vyacheslav Lozhkin, a playwright; Nikita Burkin, an acting coach; and Lyubov Arkadievna Zalesskaya, a theater critic. They were enthroned in a chamber hall at a table draped over with a velvet tablecloth the color of overripe cherries. In turn they would come out and invite the applicants. Outside, roughly twenty of us waited in the hallway, mostly students from natural sciences, mathematics, physics. I struck up a conversation with a tall, Varangian-looking fellow who kept rubbing a fur hat with tattered ear flaps against his side. His name was Pavel Mezentsev, and he immediately told me his passion was Brecht and epic theater. Next to him stood a Levantine girl, whose name was Yulia Levina. The way they gazed at each other communicated that they were in love.

The committee invited the applicants in alphabetical order, which meant that, as always, I was at the bottom of the proverbial list—still lower in Russian (ш) than in English (s). The examiners at the cherry-clothed table followed what I thought to be a script rehearsed to tiresome perfection. Lopatkin asked the main questions. From time to time, Lozhkin wedged in a hangman's joke shined by many years of use. Burkin invited the applicant to do a quick stage study of a literary character, while Lyubov Arkadievna only straightened her floral shawl and uttered occasional short phrases of commendation such as "Isn't that just marvelous?"

"And you, my dear soil scientist, what would you like to stage?" Lopatkin asked me.

Following the advice of my father, who to this day serves as my player-coach, I pitched *Eugene Onegin*.

"How lovely," Lyubov Arkadievna pronounced.

"Once again Pushkin has to bear the brunt," the corpulent Lozhkin squeezed out, dark as a storm cloud.

"Ponderous indeed," said Lopatkin, wiping his gold-rimmed spectacles. He looked like Faust playing the part of Mephistopheles. "And how exactly do you propose to do it?"

"As a Greek drama with a chorus of Russian peasant girls dressed as ladies," I explained.

After I did an impression of a gudgeon, a small over-cautious freshwater fish from the classical tale by a Russian satirist, Nikita Burkin nodded with satisfaction, and when I mentioned my former schoolmate Lyalya Telyatnikova and her project of enacting British history on stage, Lopatkin became enlivened and jotted something down in his notepad.

"Would you like to recite a couple of your poems for us?" Lopatkin asked.

"Perhaps another time," I answered.

At the end of the interviews, Burkin came out of the chamber hall and read the names of the five lucky young men and one lucky young woman who had been admitted to the Courses for Directors of the People's Theaters. I was on the list. Classes would start at the end of January 1986.

Almost immediately I knew that I hadn't just wandered into an absurd theater of the country's stagnation but into a veritable late Soviet freak show. There was no teaching plan or program whatsoever. Every Monday at seven in the evening the six of us appeared in the building of the university theater only to be passed through the same millstones. First Nikita Burkin would have us do a warm-up after Michael Chekhov's system of acting technique. When he got carried away—and he almost always did—he would start talking about a past production of Shakespeare or Racine. "When I worked at the Theater of the Moscow Soviet …," he would start in the manner of the famous actor Evstigneev but then cut himself short. The names of the professional theaters where Burkin had previously worked would change; the roles of Horatio or Orestes remained.

After that Vyacheslav Lozhkin, his gaze lowered, would go on about his own theatrical accomplishments. Even inside the theater's overheated space he did not remove his coat. His greatest success had been a production of his comedy at the Theater of the Soviet Army.

"You have no idea what went on. People would line up from the street corner to the box office," Lozhkin spoke in an underworld basso voice. "And then they shut down the production."

He permitted himself a slight degree of political innuendo, pronouncing his "g" consonant in Comrade Brezhnev's humidly fricative "Little Russian" manner. Once he even hinted that the creator of Ivan Denisovich himself had "looked favorably" upon the idea of Lozhkin's stage version of his short novel.

At the end of each class meeting, Lopatkin would announce: "And now Lyubov Arkadievna Zalesskaya is going to tell you about the Stanislavsky method."

Then Lyubov Arkadievna would appear from some secret room, where Nemirovich-Danchenko, twice the laureate of the Stalin Prize, lived and worked on his endless memoirs. In each of her monologues, Lyubov Arkadievna would quote the phrase "to become the other while remaining oneself," and this line struck me as contrary to what was happening with me and thousands of other Jewish refuseniks.

Lopatkin usually sat at the table half-turned away from us. Thumbing his silk scarf, he coughed with poise and furiously extinguished his *papirosa*. He never told stories, only giving us recommendations on what plays to read, exclusively by Western playwrights—"Pirandello, Anouilh, Dürrenmatt." And only once, as we were getting up to leave at the end of the meeting, did he say, his right hand waving off an imaginary gadfly:

"Perhaps all of you should read Arbuzov—just to get it over with. Or Afinogenov. They sure knew their stagecraft. *Mashenka* alone is worth its weight in gold …"

At the time I didn't know that *Mashenka* (Mary) was the name not only of Afinogenov's play but also of Nabokov's first novel.

Soon enough it became clear that the six of us, theatrical apprentices, were the pesky fly Lopatkin was waving off. To this day I don't understand why Lopatkin and his associates even bothered with us. They already had a student troupe of young actors and actresses, all of them aglow with thespian love and prepared to do anything only to be transformed on stage. And then there were the six of us, the inept directors of the people's theaters, six escapists and runaways.

At the end of February 1986, Lopatkin announced that we should start thinking about "certification" in June of that year. Each of us would have to direct a short production— a one-act play, a scene from a full-length one, or else an original stage adaptation. And it was assumed that actresses and actors from the university theater would be engaged in our projects. We had to present an idea to the quadrumvirate, get their blessing, and recruit performers from the university. Revisiting my *Eugene Onegin* proposal, I first suggested doing Tatiana's vatic dream before the duel and Lensky's death, but Lopatkin shot it down as "much too erotic." Then I thought of Gogol's *Inspector-General*.

"This is an eternal Russian story," I spoke out. "Don't you think very little has changed since the reign of Nicholas I? So why can't we move the action to a provincial Soviet town someplace in central or southern Russia? Dress the policemen in Soviet uniform? Instead of the charitable hospital we'll have a district clinic and so forth ..."

This was, of course, not much of an anti-Soviet affront, and yet I don't know what I expected from these conformists.

"What about naked?"

"Forgive me, Vyacheslav Mikhailovich, what do you mean?"

"Can we have the civil servants naked on stage? Isn't it what you mean?" Lozhkin asked and loudly blew his nose.

"They will most definitely not allow naked actors on stage," said the former professional actor Nikita Burkin.

It was becoming clear that taking a scene from the classical repertoire was not going to cut it. Without taking my father's advice, I decided to propose a stage interpretation of "Light Breathing," a novella by Ivan Bunin, who emigrated from Russia in 1920, settled in France, and in 1933 became the first Russian-language writer to win the Nobel Prize in Literature. I told myself that if it didn't pan out with Bunin, then it just wasn't meant to be. Why Bunin and why "Light Breathing"?

Bunin, because I admired his stories and also identified with his life in exile and his staunch anti-Bolshevism. And "Light Breathing," a novella composed and published in 1916, the last prerevolutionary year, always had a spellbinding effect on me. And I was hardly alone in thinking it a masterpiece of short fiction—Vladimir Nabokov considered "Light Breathing" an exemplary story, and Lev Vygotsky devoted a whole chapter to it in his *Psychology of Art*, impressed as he was with Bunin's nonlinear storytelling and elaborate framing. In some sense, the novella marked a breaking point in Russian classical literature—as though the "last Russian classic," as Bunin would later crown himself, refused to surrender to the torrents of modernism.

The events linked to Bunin's novella and its failed theatrical production would continue to haunt me for years, so perhaps a brief summary is in order. A meditation on life's evanescence and the destructive powers of desire, "Light Breathing" follows three interconnected episodes from the short life of Olya Meshcherskaya, a high-school queen in a small Russian city. In chronological order, the story's three main episodes are (1) Olya's seduction by her father's friend, a man much older than she; (2) Olya's tense conversation with her headmistress; and (3) Olya's eventual murder by her lover, a Cossack officer. At the very beginning of the novella, we already know Olya is dead; a cemetery scene, in which Olya's former homeroom teacher visits her grave, frames the three episodes from Olya's life. In the finale, as if lifting information from the homeroom teacher's memory, Bunin places a reflection on beauty, death, and immortality, in which Olya Meshcherskaya's *lyogkoe dykhanie* exits the confines of the fictional text: "Now her light breathing has been dispersed again in the world, in the cloudy sky, in this cold vernal wind."

I confess that in 1986 I was quite naïve about literary criticism. I just read a lot, listened, and lived by intuition. This is why I cannot vouch for the originality of the stage interpretation I proposed but only that it was entirely my own. At the heart of what I proposed to the leaders of the university theater lay the idea that on stage the events of "Light Breathing" would be narrated not by Bunin's authorial voice but by the voices of other Russian writers named in the novella. Thus Shenshin, a student at the town's classical high school who is in love with Olya Meshcherskaya, is the voice of the poet Afanasy Fet (an illegitimate son of the landowner Shenshin). And Olya Meshcherskaya herself is a descendant of Prince Meshchersky, and thus the poet Gavrila Derzhavin, Pushkin's great predecessor, would return from the dead, ascend the stage, and speak of his old friend's heiress. I described all of this quite colorfully at the next meeting, and only at the conclusion of my pitch did the devil make me boast my erudition.

"Incidentally," I said, thinking that it had gone over very well. "Incidentally, in his late collection *Dark Avenues*, Bunin would give the last name Meshchersky both to the storyteller and to his cousin, the giant whom Nathalie later marries ..."

"How very elegant of him!" said Lyubov Arkadievna.

I thought that even the misanthropic Lozhkin took to my idea.

Tossing a long grey lock off his forehead, Iosif Lopatkin turned to me, lenses of his gold-rimmed spectacles ablaze, and screamed out:

"Why in the world do you care so much about Bunin? The fascists stood at the gates of our motherland, and he sat in his villa in the Maritime Alps and wrote about naked arses."

The discussion of my project was delayed. In the meantime, I decided to test the theater's artistic director. At the next meeting, I approached Lopatkin as he stood in the foyer, smoking, and asked in a quiet voice:

"Iosif Veniaminovich, a question. Are you Jewish?"

He was taken aback at first but quickly recovered and replied so loudly that the actresses and actors standing in the theater foyer all turned in our direction:

"I happen to be a Jew, as I believe you are as well. And he," and Lopatkin spread his right arm in the direction of a tall actor with long Apollonian curls and eyes the color of prunes. "And he is a Greek. And why does it really matter? In theater, young man, there is neither Greek nor Jew. Just people on stage."

After this incident, Lopatkin stopped acknowledging me. Out of inertia I continued to attend the Monday evening classes. A Moscow March had taken possession of the city, and the streets filled with the smell of thawing earth. The other five future directors of the people's theaters were already rehearsing their productions, and I was still hoping that Lopatkin would melt swords into ploughshares and allow my production of "Light Breathing" to go forward. One evening at the end of March, the phone rang at my family's apartment not far from the Research Institute of Atomic Energy.

"This is Nikita Burkin speaking. I'm calling on behalf of the theater leadership."

"Nikita Alekseyevich, was I expelled?" I asked.

"Heavens no, quite the opposite. Iosif Veniaminovich Lopatkin requests that you join our admissions committee. We're interviewing a new group of performers."

"Forgive me, but why ask me? Don't you know that they haven't even approved my certification project …"

"Yes, but those are just temporary hurdles. You, without a doubt, show promise. That's why we'd like you to try your hand at selecting new actresses and actors. So we'll see you next Wednesday?"

"Thank you, Nikita Alekseyevich. To be honest, I was contemplating the scene of Treplyov's suicide," I said, referring to Chekhov's *The Seagull*. "A mop stick falls behind the stage. Bang—an instant death."

"Why to Yelets, Nina?" Burkin pronounced dreamily.

"I have accepted a stage engagement there for the whole winter," I sang out the words of Nina Zarechnaya in a mock falsetto.

"You, my friend, should be putting on operettas and not Chekhov," Burkin tenderly giggled into the receiver. "Well, until Wednesday."

Once again I found myself in the chamber hall of the university theater, facing the long velvet-covered table. On the table were a dusty carafe with water and a heavy ashtray (the kind Chekhov proposed improvising a story about), into which the artistic director Lopatkin now chucked his vile *papirosy*. When I entered the foyer, I saw about thirty young men and women marching in place. All of them shared the same dream: the stage, any stage. Gathered at the table were Lopatkin with a mane of silver hair and a paisley cravat, Lozhkin in a black leather coat of the sort worn by Gestapo officers in movies and buttoned to the top, Burkin in a brand-new greenish-grey tweed jacket known in Russian as "split pea print," and Lyubov Arkadievna Zalesskaya clad in a purple shawl with the customary silver fringe. Except this time, for some inexplicable reason, I was to join them at the table and sit in judgment of aspiring performers.

I was placed between Lozhkin and Zalesskaya. Burkin, who was in charge of the selection process, hurriedly explained the order of the interviews. This time they were calling the applicants not alphabetically but according to the posted sign-up sheet. The students were asked to do three things: talk about themselves, do an impression of an animal, and recite a poem or a prose excerpt.

At about eight o'clock, a tall young lady in a cornflower blue dress made of crepe de chine entered the chamber hall. I cannot say she was beautiful. But one immediately felt her breeding, a sense of finely cultivated origins. If I had seen such a young lady in the streets of Moscow, I would have first thought: "Wow, she's a tall drink of water." And then I would have noted her slender legs, narrow ankles, broad shoulders, and the emerald glimmer in her eyes. And I would have probably wanted to meet her …

"Well, tell us about yourself," Nikita Burkin suggested to the young lady, regarding her dress and matching blue shoes.

"My name is Olga Yeletskaya. I study law. More than anything in the world I love theater," said the pedigreed but unbeautiful applicant.

"Olya Yeletskaya's ruse, cry, o Soviet muse," Lozhkin muttered an improvised ditty.

"Do tell, are you descended from the princely house of Yeletsky?" Lyubov Arkadievna asked, strange hope in her voice.

Suddenly Lozhkin remembered something and livened up. "Nice town, Yelets. The Yelets Drama Theater was going to put on my comedy," he barked.

Lopatkin hungrily pulled on his *papirosa* but said nothing.

"And what kind of animal were you hoping to show us?" Burkin inquired.

"I will show you a steppe adder," Olya Yeletskaya replied.

First she sat down on the parquet floor, then prostrated herself and lay motionless for about a minute. Very slowly she began to raise her head and untangle her right hand from the restraints of her body. The hand unfolded and gyrated in the style of a periscope. A hissing, which was actually quite credible, accompanied the ascent of the head and hand.

"A nightmare," Lozhkin said rather loudly.

Olya Yeletskaya gracefully got up and bowed her head.

"Thank you. That was … That was ingenious," Burkin said. "And what text will you be reading for us?"

"I shall read an excerpt from a novella by my favorite Russian writer. You will, doubtless, soon guess who he is. I would only like to add," and Olya Yeletskaya pronounced these words in such a way that they sounded particularly authentic. "I would like to add that the author was in love with my great-grandmother."

"We're all terribly intrigued," Lyubov Arkadievna said. "Go ahead, my dear, please read."

I knew the source right away; the others had also recognized it before the excerpt gave away the title of Bunin's novella: "In one of papa's books—and he has many ancient, quaint ones—I read what kind of beauty a woman must possess ... You see, there's so much there that I couldn't remember it all: yes, definitely black eyes like boiling tar— I swear, that's exactly what it said: like boiling tar!—eyelashes black as night, a tenderly playing blush, a thin waist, arms longer than average—you get it, longer than average!" Olya Yeletskaya thus read, smoothing over the ruffles of her dress, "... a slender foot, a rather large chest, a neatly rounded calf, knees the color of seashells, downsloping shoulders—I have memorized much of it almost by heart, so it's all accurate ... But the main thing, do you know what it is? Light breathing! And I have it, just listen to the way I take my breath, don't I have it?" Olya Yeletskaya paused, as though she were listening to herself breathe.

At that moment Lopatkin slammed his open left hand on the table.

"Bunin again! Enough! This is some sort of madness," he was yelling, now turning to Olya Yeletskaya, now to me. "What in the world is wrong with you people? Don't we have other writers besides your asinine Bunin?"

"Iosif Veniaminovich, my dear, you can't do that," Lyubov Arkadievna spoke. "You'll hurt the feelings of a young gifted actress."

Olya Yeletskaya came closer to the examiners' table. Her lips trembled.

"You will live to regret this," quietly she said to Lopatkin. Then she gracefully turned around on her little heels and ran out of the chamber hall.

I caught up with her at the Manège exhibition hall, the Kremlin's crenellated walls looming ahead. Olya was sitting on the steps and weeping. Mascara trickled down her cheeks, forming a painting on her face. Winter boots jutted out of a brightly colored plastic bag of the sort many Soviet women carried along with a purse. Olya's stockinged feet were soaked from running in dress shoes over March street slush.

"You need to change. Now," I said, trying to put on the air of an older, experienced man. "And don't take this thing to heart. Big deal, some student theater …"

"For you it's not a big deal … It's not so much the theater but the way they treated me. How repulsive they are! Even the lady with the fringes …"

"About that you're right," I said, sitting down on the steps next to Olya. "I'm probably going to leave this place soon."

I told her about my fiascos and also about "naked arses."

"You're brave," Olya Yeletskaya said, tucking a braid of her hair under a hat of white mohair wool.

Wet snow started falling again.

"Let's go," I said to Olya. "I'll treat you to some *oladushki*. There's a place nearby, on Herzen Street. Maybe we'll make it."

After standing in line, we each ate a serving of chewy pancakes with thin chocolate sauce and watery coffee. It was almost nine o'clock, the café was closing. We stood at a round table by the window and stared at the city folk walking by outside.

"Listen, and about Bunin and your great-grand-mother … Is it true?" I asked.

"Of course it is. Can you imagine making this up? I was even named after her."

"That's pretty cool."

"Have you ever been to Yelets?" it was Olya's turn to ask.

"No, I haven't had the occasion."

"In Yelets the locals still call our old family mansion the 'Yeletsky house.'"

"Sounds fancy."

"It's on the former Manège Street," Olya added.

It was closing time, and the habitually angry pancake lady kicked us out of the café. Together we walked up Tverskoy Boulevard to Pushkin Square.

"Thank you, you're very nice," Olya said.

She kissed me on the cheek and ran down the steps into the metro station. I didn't go down into the metro. Instead, I walked over to my friend Methodius's place. He lived in a communal apartment on Petrovka Street just a few blocks from Pushkin Square and kept an open house with drinks, *zakuski*, and a boombox ...

The following day, at about 10 p.m., Olya Yeletskaya telephoned.

"I didn't wake you, did I?"

"Of course not."

"You know," Olya said a bit nervously. "I was brought up this way ... If I like someone or something, I don't know how to hide it."

Feeling trapped, I said nothing.

"Let's go out," Olya suggested. "I like you a lot."

"Olya, I'm actually seeing someone," I answered a half-truth. "You see, it's serious …"

From the red receiver came some hissing, and then Olya's angry words followed:

"You will regret it, my dear. I don't tolerate refusals."

She said exactly that and slammed down the receiver. The reason I still remember it verbatim was the word "refusal," which at the time held a special meaning for my family.

First the falling out with Lopatkin and then the encounter with Olya Yeletskaya pushed me to withdraw from the Courses for Directors of the People's Theaters. In the spring of 1986, the refuseniks' political theater drew me into its street and apartment performances, while writing poetry became my principal métier. I managed to last until April, then left and never again showed my face at the university theater located at the corner of Herzen and Mokhovaya Streets. Like Chekhov's hopeful bride, I left thinking that I would never again return to this theatrical story with the young Princess Yeletskaya, her great-grandmother, and the writer Ivan Bunin.

Over thirty years went by. At this point, I had already lived in Boston for as long as I had once lived in Moscow. I was teaching at a liberal arts college, writing books, and traveling. I married on the late side. My wife, a physician, the daughter of a Jewish man originally from North Bukovina and a Jewish woman originally from South Africa, did not grow up with a lot of Russian culture. My wife's father used to tell his kids that if he went back to Czernowitz, they would make him a doctor in the Russian army. He also taught them the Russian word for strawberry, *klubnika*. My wife and I visited Russia during our honeymoon, but after that she didn't feel a need to join me on my regular trips back. Russia hadn't touched her heart the way Brazil, France, or Italy did. She accepted my Russian—Soviet—background as a given yet belonged to the category of people who take care not to repeat the mistakes of Lot's wife and of Euridice, which is why they didn't look back and lived by—for—the present and future. Unlike my wife, I was still held captive by memories of my Soviet years. And our American children had inherited both my wife's talent for letting go and my own knack for clinging on to the past.

Now and again, I would run into Soviet phantoms, though it was a bit surprising that only once did I cross paths with the people I used to know at the university theater back in Moscow. This happened in Israel, in January 2014. I was speaking at the Jerusalem Russian Library. A powerfully built man wearing a white-and-blue woven *kippah*, his full round beard the color of ripe wheat, came up to me after my talk. A petite woman in an ankle-length skirt, strands of thick, salty black hair refusing to stay under her headscarf, stood beside him.

"Do you remember us?" asked the bearded man.

"Your faces look familiar," I replied. "But I'm not quite sure ..."

"January '86, Herzen Street ... Remember now?"

They were Pavel Mezentsev and Yulia Levina, who were in the same cohort as I was at the Courses for Directors of the

People's Theaters. The Varangian boy and Levantine girl who so adored Brecht ...

Nothing should surprise an ex-Soviet, including the fact that in 1991 Pavel (who was not Jewish when I met him in Moscow) and Yulia (who was Jewish yet showed no interest in her origins) made aliyah. They became settler activists. Pavel's first name was now Shaul. He and his wife had five children.

"I sleep with a submachine gun," Pavel said, smiling broadly.

"You know, we have your books at home," Yulia added.

"Guys, what about your theater work?" I asked.

"Youthful illusions," Pavel answered. Yulia quietly nodded.

"That's very true," I said.

We stood in the middle of the library floor.

"By the way, do you remember Lopatkin, the artistic director?" I asked for no apparent reason.

"Of course we do, are you kidding?" Yulia said. "You left, but we ... we stayed and worked at the theater for three more years. As Lopatkin's assistants."

"Didn't he become quite successful in the late 1980s?" I asked.

"He did. One of perestroika's heroes. He was put in charge of his own professional theater. Staged a play about Stalin that half of Moscow saw. Became a People's Artist of Merit," Pavel-Shaul said with pride.

"And then," Yulia added. "And then his life ended."

We exchanged contacts and said goodbye. In the evening, when I got back to my hotel room in Rechavia, I googled Lopatkin's name and quickly came upon an announcement that in March 1999 "the distinguished figure of the Russian theater, director, and teacher Iosif Veniaminovich Lopatkin was killed with a pistol shot in the entryway of his apartment building near Dynamo Stadium. The murder is under investigation. The funeral service will take place at the Church of All Saints …"

* * *

In the spring of 2019 I started to prepare for my annual summer trip to Russia. The third edition of my book about Bunin and Nabokov had just come out, and I was looking forward to readings in Moscow and St. Petersburg. For many years I had been bringing my daughters along on my summer pilgrimages to Russia, and it was my younger, Tanyusha's, turn.

Every time we journeyed to Russia, I tried to show my daughters not only new parts of Moscow and St. Petersburg but also a slice of antiquated life, pockets of the past that had survived and remained more or less the same as I had once seen them as a university student, when I fell in love with rural Russia. This time I had decided to visit the places of Ivan Bunin's youth, which lay in the Tula, Lipetsk, and Oryol provinces south of Moscow. I was contemplating a short biography of the great writer, and how could one imagine Bunin the teenager, Bunin the dropout from the classical high school, without traveling to the towns of Efremov and

Yelets? Everything was working out so well as I prepared to travel to Russia on the eve of Bunin's sesquicentennial. I was even invited to give a talk in the Bunin museum in Efremov, in the former house of his older brother Evgeny, and also a guest lecture at Yelets State University. Our local hosts promised guided tours, a "cultural program" …

Here I should explain that annual summer trips weren't just an opportunity to show different parts of Russia to my daughters. For me these visits were also a return to my own childhood and youth—the lost joy of pure friendship. In the wrong place yet at the right time. Joining me on the annual trips to one historic site or another were my dear friends Lena Kogan and Max Krolik. We had met as children in the early 1970s. On our annual pilgrimages—to Dostoevsky's Staraya Russa or to the Pskov Province where Pushkin had spent his northern exile—I felt not only like an American father and immigrant of many years but also like a teenager who had never parted with Russia.

On a hot morning in July 2019, we got into a large black SUV with three rows of seats, left Moscow, and drove south in the direction of Tolstoy's ancestral lands. Our party was composed of three generations: Lena, a philanthropist and founder of one of the first private assisted living facilities in Russia, was driving the black SUV; next to Lena, a driving map in hand, sat Alechka, Max Krolik's second wife, a screenwriter; slouched in the second row were Krolik and I, sipping Old Königsberg, a Russian-bottled cognac, and chasing it with bitter Russian chocolate by the name of *Vdokhnovenie* (Inspiration); my younger daughter, having claimed the whole third row, was left to her own—electronic—devices. Lena, Krolik, and I were all in our fifties; Alechka was a little over thirty; Tanyusha was eleven. Three generations of those who travel by land …

At around one in the afternoon, we drove into Efremov, a tidy provincial town, where decay didn't hit you in the face, and the air was scented with ironweed, sawwort, and other flowers of the forest steppe. The museum occupied a brick mansard house, its walls the color of dark red coral. One Bunin monument stood in front of the street entrance, the other in the fenced courtyard surrounding the annex.

An attractive woman wearing a white blouse and a scarlet skirt ran out the door and greeted us. She introduced herself as head curator.

"So happy you're here," she said. "We've all been on pins and needles. Everything is completely ready."

We asked where we could get lunch. The museum worker gave us walking directions to Tomato Café—straight on Turgenev Street, past the high school, then down Sverdlov

Street. We invited her to join us for lunch as our guest, and she replied, with much dignity:

"Thank you, but I just got up from the table."

This sounded like a phrase from a faraway past ...

About sixty people came to hear my talk. They included teachers, musicians, local authors and visual artists, and even a regional benefactor of the museum, a man with a Germanic last name. A whole clan of Bunin's relatives via his brother Evgeny was there in attendance, all of them resembling the writer Bunin. Genes eternal ...

I hadn't enjoyed a reading or talk so much in a very long time. First a trio of local musicians, teachers at the Efremov School of Music—chromatic button accordion, violin, and viola—performed Astor Piazzolla tunes. Then the director of the museum spoke about my family, our lives before and after emigration, and showed photos she had found on the internet. It was very touching and only a tiny bit embarrassing. After the introduction I talked about the great rivalry of Bunin and Nabokov, and at the end Tanyusha and I signed copies of my books. There was only one jarring moment. During the questions, a female voice asked a question from the very back of the museum's parlor:

"Professor, what is your position regarding the return of the Bunin papers from England to Russia, the great writer's homeland?"

It was so crowded I couldn't see the woman who posed the question. And I really didn't feel like getting into it and upsetting the spirit of the gathering. I made an effort and replied:

"As far as I know, the papers were donated to Leeds University by the writer's legitimate heirs. We're here to celebrate the art of Ivan Alekseevich Bunin."

And that's where I left it. The museum's director, as far as I could tell, sensed my reluctance and steered the conversation away from controversy. Afterward some of the guests and all the staff members went out into the courtyard to take a group photo. I sent Tanyusha ahead with Lena and lingered behind, hoping to take another look at the room where Bunin's mother spent her last days.

"Excuse me, professor," the head curator approached me. "I would like you to meet a great friend of our museum."

I turned around. A tall stately woman of about fifty stood in the doorway. She wore an elegant if conservative skirt suit made of thin wool the color of ripe cherries. A cream-colored high-necked silk blouse could be seen under her jacket. Her lustrous, chestnut hair was carefully arranged into a double bun. A string of large pinkish pearls hung around her neck. In her right hand, she held an expensive-looking briefcase of yellow leather.

The head curator ceremoniously introduced the tall lady:

"This is Olga Vikentievna Yeletskaya, senior state councilor of the Russian Federation. She does so much for the development of museums and archives in our country. And especially for Bunin's heritage."

"We've actually met," said the lady from my Soviet past. "Don't you recognize me, dear professor?"

"Of course I do," I answered.

"Oh, forgive me please … I had no idea you knew each other," the nice museum worker sounded flustered.

"We have long been following your publications, professor," said Olga Yeletskaya. "We follow them, and we value the fact that even though you left Russia, you have remained a friend of Russian culture."

Olga hadn't, in fact, changed much. She had the air of Russian imperial self-importance. I immediately thought of Hélène Kuragin's "alabaster breast" from *War and Peace*. Hadn't they taught us well in Soviet schools—all to their own detriment?

Luckily for me, my daughter ran into the room and pulled me into the courtyard, where the museum staff and the local intelligentsia were posing in three undulating rows in front of the bronze bust of Bunin. We came out of the museum annex and stood next to Lena and Krolik; Olga Yeletskaya followed and stood in the front row, just left of Bunin.

At first I hadn't given much thought to Olga's appearance on my horizon, just as I wouldn't give much thought to dark patterns on the surface of the Moon. I would certainly never have connected my talk at the Bunin museum in Efremov with the restoration of an old theatrical affair.

In the meantime, we said goodbye to Efremov and its inhabitants and loaded ourselves into the black SUV.

"What was *that* all about?" Lena asked me.

"It's practically a movie script: While traveling across the rural Russia of Bunin's youth, a Russian-American writer and scholar encounters his old flame," commented Alechka.

"Have a sip of cognac. Let's toast your victory," said Krolik, taking out the half-empty flat bottle and a new chocolate bar.

"Cut it out, people, seriously. What flame? If anything, she's a flame extinguisher. To be honest, I'd forgotten all about her. Until now, that is …"

The crème-indigo-and-gold Ascension Cathedral soared over Yelets. A band played in the town's pleasure garden, where young ladies on dates with young men walked with pride, and happy Russian families strolled along the shady alleys. We were staying at the Larks Hotel on Lenin Street (the former Manège Street). The hotel was in a two-story stone mansion with a cast-iron entrance and overhang. The mansion's ornate window trim and eaves were painted white. Walking from the reception area toward a back staircase with carved balustrades, we saw, occupying a place of honor on the wall of the guest parlor, a large portrait of Stalin in the uniform of the Marshal of the Soviet Union.

"Why do you have that painting here?" I asked the receptionist who was about to show us to our rooms.

"This happens to be a painting by a local artist. Our owner collects them," she replied. "Everything you see here on the walls is by local Yelets masters."

"Excuse me," Alechka inquired. "Could you tell us who the owner is?"

"You know, she doesn't like to advertise her name …"

"Well, perhaps you could give us a hint?" I asked.

"This building used to be their ancestral mansion," the reception lady answered with pride. "Our owner, she reclaimed it, had it all restored to its original design and pre-Revolutionary style. They even come here to shoot pictures."

"And your Stalin, he's also from before the revolution?" Alechka asked.

119

We decided to change and go out for dinner. I came down a few minutes before the others, removed the portrait of the murderer of nations from the wall and placed it under the main staircase. Later in the evening, when we came back to the hotel after dinner, a different painting was hanging in place of Stalin's portrait—a vase with golden elongated grapes, blushing apples and smokey pears.

"That was fast," Krolik pointed out, and we parted until morning.

The following day was so full that I still don't understand where I got the energy to go on a nighttime expedition which nearly led to a disaster. In the morning I gave a lecture at the local university—the I. A. Bunin Yelets State University, formerly a teacher's college. Then Professor Ivan Borisovich I., an expert in émigré poetry, walked me back to the hotel, where my daughter and friends were waiting, having already visited the souvenir stores on Mira ("Peace") Street, formerly Kupecheskaya ("Merchant") Street. My daughter bought some of the famed Yelets lace for her school and camp girlfriends, and Lena purchased a trove of local crafts to decorate the rooms at her sanatorium. Most of the day was taken up by a walking tour of Yelets and a drive to the homesteads of Butyrki and Ozyorki, which Bunin's family once owned. Our tour guide, a historian of Yelets and its environs, was a lecturer at the university.

For me the tour started and ended at the Yelets Women's High School. This doesn't mean I ignored the town's other attractions. I dutifully photographed the old cemetery, which

Bunin describes in "Light Breathing," the cottage where young Bunin lived as a boarder while attending the Yelets Men's Classical High School (which produced a number of distinguished graduates, including Nikolai Semashko, the future People's Commissar of Health), the drama theater (which Chekhov mentions in *The Seagull*), and even the house-museum of the famous Soviet composer Tikhon Khrennikov. But for me the prism of the whole story, through which the prospect of an entirely different finale was oneirically revealed, was the Yelets Women's High School.

This edifice of three stories was built in the 1870s with such thought and care that it survived the revolution and civil war, the wartime bombings of the town located close to the front line, and the peripeteia of postwar Soviet living. The worker's college, which later grew into the teacher's university, used to have its offices and classrooms here. When we toured the former Yelets Women's High School, silence reigned in its halls—either a major renovation was about to start, or the former occupants were moving to the main campus. I was most struck by the gorgeous one-piece cast-iron staircase, its balustrades a masterwork of iron lace.

"How could they afford such fancy décor?" Lena asked our tour guide.

"My dear lady, you probably don't know this," the guide answered with adorned pride. "Yelets used to be one of Russia's wealthiest small cities. Our grain merchants were famous all over the empire. We had the country's first grain elevator built in 1888. Imagine that!"

We roamed around the building, at random entering former department offices and auditoria, now emptied of furniture. A young lady with "light breathing," Olya Meshcherskaya in Bunin's story, once attended this women's high school. Something led me to a classroom, one of its long walls lined with tall bookcases with glass doors standing atop cabinets with solid wooden doors. Stored inside the glass bookcases were old teaching materials. I saw blazing red bindings, the bleeding covers of old books. The bookcases and cabinets were not only locked with a key but also protected by horizontal strips of paper with stamped clay seals. I pulled on the doorknobs of the cabinets and brushed my right thumb across the polished wood, collecting a thick layer of dust. I couldn't shake the thought of undoing the locks, breaking the seals, and getting inside the bookcases and cabinets. For the rest of the day, I fought myself and kept losing to temptation. I realized it was sheer madness. And yet I knew that I would find what I was looking for ...

In the evening, our party had dinner at a restaurant located across from the Ascension Cathedral. Krolik and I had a lot of vodka—more than I ever drink at home in America. When we got back to the hotel my daughter fell asleep right away, whereas I had an attack of insomnia. I read until late before I finally dozed off. Then I woke up and wrote two notes by the light of the iPhone. One of them I placed on the side table at the head of my daughter's bed: "Tanyusha, if I'm not here when you wake up, go to Lena's room. Love, Papa." The other note, in Russian, was for Lena herself: "I'll explain everything later. Stay with Tanyusha. Don't leave the hotel without her. Kisses, M." I quietly got dressed and left the room. On the way downstairs I placed the note under Lena's door.

I stole into the basement, opened the mechanical room, took two screwdrivers and a pair of pliers, and buried the tools in the deep side pocket of my military-style tunic known in Russian as *french*—after the British Field Marshal John Denton Pinkstone French. The screwdrivers and pliers jingled in my pocket. I tiptoed up the stairs and left through the back door, where Lena's black SUV was parked. It was a brisk walk of about ten minutes from the hotel to the building of the former Yelets Women's High School. The front door was locked. I looked both ways over my shoulder, removed a flat screwdriver from my pocket and jimmied the lock open. I was surprised by the ease with which it gave. Having snuck inside the building, I ran down the corridor and entered the last classroom on the first floor. I stopped, catching my breath. Where to begin?

I saw a stack of bound notebooks in one of the glass bookcases. Breaking a slender lock, I started leafing through the contents. Those were senior theses by philology students from the 1930s. Like a gambler, his body hovering over the roulette table, desperate but unable to place his bet, I kept turning my gaze from one cabinet to the next. My hands were shaking. "What the hell is wrong with you? Stop before it's too late," I tried to reason with myself, but all in vain. In turn, I kept breaking open the doors of the cabinets and examining their contents. There was a lot of curious stuff there—very old textbooks, primers and dictionaries; rulers, compasses, and copper inkwells. In one cabinet I found bound issues of *Niva* (Virgin Soil), a magazine from the 1880s. But I was searching for something else, something I wasn't finding. It was already past 3 a.m. I was nervous about getting back to the hotel but couldn't stop.

Three unopened cabinets remained in the darkest, farthest corner of the classroom, where neither the summer moonlight nor the glow of streetlamps could reach. I sat on the floor in front of the middle of the remaining three cabinets, stuck the blade of the screwdriver under the heart of the lock and pulled on the door. On the middle shelf there were notebooks that looked old. In my head I called them "journals." Dusting off the covers, I was able to make out the names of the young ladies who attended the high school. There were about fifty notebooks. Taking a chance, I pulled six notebooks from the middle, spread them before me and started examining them. I wasn't even that surprised when I saw, written by a determined hand, the name "Olga Yeletskaya" and the year "1886." The notebook was half-filled with some French passages, which would have taken me a while to read. At the end of the notebook, I located a page folded into a corner. On the back of the corner: the words "Ваня Бунинъ" (Vanya Bunin) and beneath them, drawn in a fine ink pen, a cupid holding a bow and arrow. Four more pages followed, filled with small, elegant Russian lines and divided into paragraphs, each opening with a date. It looked like a diary hidden in the depths of a school exercise notebook. I took out my iPhone and, feeling something close to ecstasy, photographed the title page, the leather binding, the corner, and the drawing with the name of the great Russian writer placed above the flying cupid. Having made sure that the flash worked sufficiently, I aimed to fit an entire page of the notebook and began the scanning of the diary pages.

Suddenly a blinding light washed over me. I turned and saw Olga Yeletskaya, frozen in the classroom doorway. Over the cherry business suit, she wore a beige belted trench coat with epaulettes. Two gaping police officers, a lieutenant and a sergeant, stood behind Yeletskaya's back.

"Well, professor, just as expected ...," she said loudly. I was silent, my eyes still adjusting to the light after several hours in the dark.

"Did you think you were getting away with this?" Yeletskaya asked.

"I wasn't thinking anything," I answered. "I just wanted to know the truth behind the fiction."

"And so now you do!" she said in a triumphal voice.

"Go ahead," she ordered the policemen, her voice vibrating with power. "Start the processing protocol. Forced entry. Broken front door lock. Broken book-cases and cabinets. Official seals. And don't forget the fingers ..."

"Olya, do you remember how back in '86 you did an impression of a steppe adder?" I asked, addressing her with the familiar *ty* pronoun.

"Leave us," she ordered the two policemen. "Close the door and wait outside."

Olga Yeletskaya approached me, softly stepping on the old parquet floor.

"Why did you come here?" she asked. "Why would you even want to come back to Russia? We don't need you here, do you understand? We-do-not-need-you."

"Yes, I understand, Olga Vikentievna, I understand everything," I said and suddenly felt with the utmost clarity that I had to escape from there and rescue my child, no matter the cost.

"Hand me your smartphone, professor," said Yeletskaya.

She erased all the photos and scans of her great-grandmother's notebook before she handed the phone back to me.

"By the way, I haven't finished reading your great-grandmother's diary," I said.

"I don't know what you're talking about. Now give me the notebook," Olga Yeletskaya all but ordered me.

She lowered the notebook into her leather briefcase, closed the clasps, and smiled with malice.

"You took pity on me back in 1986," she said. "At that idiotic theater audition. And then you took pity on me again—when you turned me down. Now we're even, professor, doubly even. Go, I'm not keeping you."

"Aren't you going to bring up the Jews who abandoned Russia on the brink of disaster?" I asked, unable to hold back.

"I was raised not to say certain things out loud," Princess Yeletskaya sliced. "Go now!"

Legs wobbly, I walked toward the door. My hand already on the ornate door handle, I turned back and asked Yeletskaya:

"And the notebook, you'll surely hide it in some secret vault? Or will you destroy it?"

Olga Yeletskaya, senior state councilor of the Russian Federation, turned her gaze from the bookcases and cabinets to the yellow windows of the former Yelets Women's High School.

"Leave and do not come back," she said sternly. Then she looked me in the eye and added: "Ever!"

I walked past the uncomprehending police officers. At daybreak I ran down the streets of Yelets.

Tanyusha was still asleep when I got back, innocent of her father's transgressions. I set the alarm for 8 a.m. and fell back asleep.

At breakfast I announced to my friends that something very strange had happened overnight and our plans had changed.

"I'll tell you everything, but a little later. Now just trust me, my dears. This is for the better …"

We packed hastily, forgetting the plastic bag with the lace of Yelets on the table in our hotel room. We loaded into the black SUV and sped off, not to the great city of Oryol, where we had been planning to conclude our journey through Bunin's Russia, but back to Moscow.

The next morning my daughter and I left on the first flight to Amsterdam.

A Return to Kafka

That case, demonstrating the mysterious metamorphosis of the cockchafer, inspired Fritz and me in the late spring to an intensive study of the whole nature of cockchafers, including anatomical examination and culminating in the cooking and eating of a cockchafer stew.

—W. G. Sebald, tr. Michael Hulse

In the fall of 1989, two American years tucked under my Soviet-made leather belt, I was getting a master's degree in comparative literature and trying to figure out how to become an academic without having to strangle my literary ambitions. Paths of Russian poetry brought me to Konstantin Konstantinovich Kuzminsky (Russian moniker "KKK"), poet, anthologist, and performance artist, who was born in Leningrad in 1940, emigrated in 1975, first lived in Austin, Texas, then subsequently in Brooklyn for many years, and died in the hamlet of Lordville, NY, near the New York-Pennsylvania border in 2015. He was a living legend made up of poetic hyperbole and prosaic contradiction. At the time I got to know him, Kuzminsky held court not far from Brighton Beach, in the basement of an inelegant apartment building that he, his wife, Emma (Russian moniker "Mysh'" ["Mouse"]), and several greyhounds were renting

129

in addition to a small first-floor apartment. Kuzminsky's *Podval* (Basement) was one of the centers of New York's émigré cultural life, a combination of salon, gallery, and reading venue. Bearded and long-haired, witty, and ardently committed to living the life of a bohemian, Kuzminsky spent his days and nights lying on a bed in various robes worn over his puffy naked body, collecting and disseminating Russian poetry, and receiving visitors in his underground abode, its walls decorated with avant-garde art, anarchist flags, and antique weapons.

My father and Kuzminsky knew each other slightly through the Leningrad poetry connection, and I once brought my parents to Kuzminsky's basement for a visit. Kuzminsky's great contribution was the multivolume *Blue Lagoon Anthology of Modern Russian Poetry*, which he spearheaded, coedited, and never completed.

Kuzminsky was generous, vulnerable, and creatively bigoted. Although not a Jew himself, he was surrounded by mostly men and women who had come to America on the wings of the great Jewish emigration. Jewish questions somehow bothered and irked him, perhaps in spite of his own better judgement. "I walk on the low verge of the forbidden," he once told me, recalling a comment he had made in one of his publications. The comment had to do with with the blood libel. Referring to two immigrant brothers, his former landlords, Kuzminsky stated that Jews "drink blood … have drunk two buckets of my own blood." But Kuzminsky also admired and promoted Jewish poets, including those who made aliyah and were living in Israel. Among them was the Jewish avant-gardist mystic Ilia Bokstein, who published a long illuminated manuscript of his own poems, *Glints of the Wave*, and died outside Tel Aviv in 1999. In the days of my literary youth, I enjoyed Kuzminsky's kindness and even borrowed a couple of tricks from his old fedora.

It was Kuzminsky who infected me with an anti-Kafkian germ, and the germ stayed in my system for three decades.

"What sort of books do you read in your graduate courses?" Kuzminsky asked me in December 1989.

I was taking a seminar on the novel, and *The Trial* was on the syllabus.

"Do you like Kafka?" Kuzminsky asked, disappointment in his voice.

"Less than Joyce or Proust," I gave a safe answer.

A tirade followed, in which Kuzminsky explained that he divided writers into "Kafkians" and "Rabelaisians." Kafkians, he said, were cerebral, sickly, darkly shaded, depressing, sparsely worded. Rabelaisians were exuberant, carnal, sunny, verbally inventive.

"Many Jews are Kafkians," he said.

"What about Babel? Chagall?" I objected.

"Those are exceptions," Kuzminsky stated. And then he asked in exasperation: "Why do American intellectuals love the term 'Kafkaesque' so much? Everything is Kafkaesque to them. How would they know? At least we have our communal apartments … well, the KGB, for Pete's sakes."

For years I appreciated Kafka but kept my distance. I taught him on occasion, and I even published a bit on Nabokov's visits to Prague and his begrudgingly acknowledged debt to Kafka. But Kafka wasn't a writer I loved or read for pleasure. And the ex-Soviet in me never got into the habit of throwing the term "Kafkaesque" left and right—like the red badge of confusion. And then, in the winter of 2021, a pandemic-driven attempt to wrest a honorarium from a Russian publisher made me rethink my relationship with the great Jewish modernist from Prague.

For many years, I had been going to Russia once, sometimes twice, a year—usually in early summer and late fall. And I would devote one day to visiting publishers in order to collect literary earnings. These royalties and honoraria weren't substantial, and especially so when converted from rubles to dollars. But they were sufficient to buy presents for my wife, children, and parents and to have some pocket money while I was in Russia. More recently, I would invite my daughters along when I visited Moscow on royalty-collecting trips around the city. And I would tell them of the good-bad old Soviet days, when my father used to take me with him to editorial offices and treat me to something delicious like a smoked tongue sandwich with pear soda after receiving honoraria.

With the onset of COVID-19, I stopped traveling. Royalties for three of my Russian books were accumulating, however, and I resolved to collect them without leaving Boston. Two publishers readily agreed to wire me the funds, whereas the third one refused. The publisher's business office wrote to me that other than collecting the royalties in person, I had the option to create something called a "Yandex purse," to which they would periodically deposit my earnings. In the original Russian, *yandeks koshelek* sounds a bit oxymoronic, as though a Victorian lady were to rise from the grave and start an advertising agency.

I shared the news with my very wise mother.

"That bureaucratic country is beyond change," she said. "Why do you need it?"

"These are my rightful earnings," I responded.

"Don't get involved," my mother cautioned me. "There's a reason we left Russia for good. I worry every time you go back there."

As usual, I didn't take my mother's advice. "Yes," I said, "a major pain in the butt. And I've got to figure it out."

Having signed up for a "Yandex purse," I sent the information to my publisher's business office. The next day they replied: "You have signed up for an 'anonymous purse.'

What we need from you is an 'identified purse.'" A scent of death emanated from my desktop screen. I read the rules on the Yandex site. In order to register for an "identified purse," one would either need to appear in person at one of their offices in Russia or send by certified mail an application, a copy of one's passport, and a translation of the entire paperwork. At this point I already knew this was going to be complicated, and I turned to their online support for assistance.

The following day I received this response via email (here and hereafter are my literal translations from the Russian):

Hello!
For sending copies of documents by mail, you can notarize your signature, and since we understand that your documents will not be in the Russian language, you need to put an apostille on the documents.
Detailed instructions are found here: https://yoomoney.ru/page?id=536164
When we receive and process your data, a notification will appear in your purse. You will need to check the information, and, if everything is correct, your purse will immediately become identified.
With respect,
Natalia
User support service

I needed further clarification. Again I emailed Yandex user support: "Please tell me, does the application form require an apostille? And is a translation of the passport needed?"

An hour later I received a response, in which the possessives refused to get along:

Hello.
Apostille is placed on the notary's passport's attestation.
You must have a copy of your passport notarized, then have an apostille placed on the notary's attestation, then take it to a translation service and have them translate the passport, attestation, and apostille. Thereafter the translator's signature must also be notarized.
With respect,
Artyom
User support service

I felt the beginning of an existential crisis, hence this next email that I dispatched to Yandex user support: "Ladies and gentlemen, I do not understand. What in the passport requires translation? In my (US) passport I have a Russian visa in Russian. Perhaps that would suffice? Or I could translate it myself. I am a professor of Russian literature. And I could obtain a university seal. Thank you."

The next response arrived literally in minutes. It was detailed, unrelenting, and resembled a Minotaur's labyrinth:

> *Hello.*
>
> *For all foreign citizens, if in any type of document the data is not given in parallel Russian, an official translation of this document is required. This same translation must be notarized. If the attestation is also in a foreign language, then a translation is also required.*
>
> *The translation must be carried out by an official translation bureau. Your own translation of your own documents (arbitrary translation) or the notary's translation of his own attestation is not permitted.*
>
> *With respect,*
>
> *Vasilisa,*
>
> *User support service*

I printed out the "identified purse" application, made a copy of my passport. Then I googled a Russian translation agency and found one located in Boston. I called, a woman with an accent answered. I switched to Russian. The woman spoke in a confident voice with a southern Russian pronunciation. She explained that her office used to be in Boston but has since moved to Minnesota.

"Scan and text me the papers, I'll look them over and take care of it for you," she offered.

But I first needed to have the application and passport copy notarized, then have an apostille placed on them at the office of the secretary of state (its own bureaucratic morass). I was still determined to complete the task, however hopeless it may have already appeared.

I made an appointment at a local branch of Bank of America.

"Are you here to open an account?" asked the banker, an immigrant from South Asia.

"No, I'm here to have a couple of things notarized, I already have an account here."

"We do not notarize passport copies," said the banker. "And I cannot notarize your application because there's no notary block on it."

"Couldn't you make an exception?" I asked.

"I can't, I'm sorry. I deal with this all the time," she answered.

I returned home and emailed a plea for help to Yandex user support service: "Sirs, what you ask for cannot be accomplished in the US. Here they do not notarize passport copies. And the application also could not be notarized because there is no notary block on it. I don't know what to do."

A reply from Russia arrived in the evening:

Hello.
We understand that you have found yourself in a difficult situation, but our rules are mandatory for all users.

We cannot accept unnotarized documents or your signature on the application.
We cannot make an exception for you. We recommend doing what we wrote to you in prior letters—that is the only way of resolving your matter.
With respect,
Ekaterina
User support service

I came out of my home office, walked over to a bookcase, my feet unsteady, and took out a copy of Kafka's *The Trial*. It's been at my bedside ever since—next to my wife's photograph, a paperback edition of *Tanakh* and an old *Farmer's Almanac*.

THE END

Acknowledgements

I am deeply grateful to Boston College for supporting my work over the past twenty-seven years. I would also like to express my great appreciation to the editors of the magazines in which earlier versions of some of the pages of this book originally appeared in English or Russian. Dobrochna Fire copyedited the manuscript with her impeccable sense of structure and with tolerance of the author's follies. Stuart Allen prepared the manuscript for publication and offered further stylistic wisdom.

As always, the staff of Academic Studies Press has been welcoming and enthusiastic, and I would especially like to thank Alessandra Anzani, Matthew Charlton, Ivan Grave, Becca Kearns, and Kira Nemirovsky.

* * *

Without the love and support of my wife Karen, daughters Mira and Tatiana, and parents Mila and David, there would have been no Venice of my dreams, no adventures, and no book about dreams and adventures.

Last but not least, many translingual barks of pleasure go to Stella the real star.

Index of Names and Places

Photo: Lee Pellegrini

Maxim D. Shrayer, bilingual author and scholar, was born in Moscow in 1967 to a Jewish-Russian family with Ukrainian and Lithuanian roots and spent over eight years as a refusenik. He and his parents, the writer David Shrayer-Petrov and the translator Emilia Shrayer, left the USSR and immigrated to the United States in 1987. Shrayer received a PhD from Yale University in 1995. He is Professor of Russian, English, and Jewish Studies at Boston College. Shrayer has authored and edited over twenty books of nonfiction, criticism, fiction, poetry, and translations. Among his books are the literary memoirs *Waiting for America* and *Leaving Russia* and the collection *A Russian Immigrant: Three Novellas.* He is the recipient of a number of awards and fellowships, including a 2007 National Jewish Book Award and a 2012 Guggenheim Fellowship. Shrayer's publications have been translated into ten languages. He lives in Massachusetts with his wife, Dr. Karen E. Lasser, a medical researcher and physician, and their daughters Mira and Tatiana.

Printed in the USA
CPSIA information can be obtained
at www.ICGtesting.com
JSHW050924311023
51111JS00031B/85